MW01042932

Spectral Realms

No. 8 ‡ Winter 2018

Edited by S. T. Joshi

The spectral realms that thou canst see
With eyes veil'd from the world and me.

H. P. LOVECRAFT, "To a Dreamer"

SPECTRAL REALMS is published twice a year by Hippocampus Press, P.O. Box 641, New York, NY 10156 (www.hippocampuspress.com).
Cover art "Cave Dwellers" by Mutartis Boswell.
Cover design by Barbara Briggs Silbert.
Hippocampus Press logo by Anastasia Damianakos.

ISBN: 978-1-61498-219-7   ISSN 2333-4215

Contents

Poems

Through Druid Oaks

Leigh Blackmore

(*For Victor H. Anderson*)

With scarlet veins your opalescent robe
Is threaded through; the sacred silver groves
Lie still; the moon, an iridescent globe
Illumines earth that hides old treasure troves.

Through druid oaks, their catkins full and wide,
You roam, enraptured, seeking for the shrine
Of Cailleach where sense and soul might guide
Your future way—ill-fated borderline.

Forbidden hungers—feathers of dark wings—
Phantasmal lusts brush on your lips unkissed.
Your breasts as ripe delightsome fruit, that kings
Might pluck from laden boughs with languid wrist.

Now sombre shadows fall and you behold
My dark-robed presence stalking through the wood.
The shadows lengthen, as was long foretold.
Strange melodies ring out, for womanhood.

Your lantern light unmasked and held on high
Now stays my step, as taken unawares,
I find myself held fast 'twixt truth and lie.
Now who stalks who in answer to whose prayers?

Yet still your lithe and lovely limbs' caress
Inflames my body; burning with desire,
Your lips I kiss. To you I acquiesce,
Perfervid; and my veins run with red fire

As in my neck, where beating pulses swell,
(So tempting, yielding, soft) you sink your fangs.
This tryst has proven naught but my death-knell:
Another of *your* daily new birth pangs.

Belladonna

Abigail Wildes

So sweet the blackened berry,
    Upon the child's small lips.
And it flows into the bloodstream,
    In poisoned little sips.

To drain the cheeks of color,
    And still those eyes of blue.
Will stop the heart of innocence,
    Before they even knew.

Such pretty little flowers,
    That the Devil claims his own.
And pretty little berries,
    To take the child home.

His mother's screams are muted,
    As a father shakes the boy.
But there is nothing left of him,
    Save black berries by a toy.

The Flitter-Bird and the Bloom of Doom

Richard L. Tierney

My lovely humming bird, you're such a swift and fickle flitterer,
Darting among the garden blooms, a rapid, squeaky chitterer,
Sucking the nectar from each generous flower's sweet and open heart.
Then, when that savory nectar's spent, you feel it's time for you to part.
You flitter on capriciously to suck your next sweet donor's draught,
Then you dart most erratically—left-right, up-downward, fore and aft.
You love to flaunt your deft maneuvers to the wondering viewer's sight.
No speedy hawk can hope to snatch you in your rapid zigzag flight.
And yet—Beware, sweet flitterer! The planet's climate is fast changing.
Gardens grow swampy now while strange new seeds and spores, far ranging
On tropic winds, into our fields and flower beds are deftly sown.
Their shoots appear, expanding quickly into exotic blooms full grown.
Their multicolored petals flare alluringly
And from their throats there floats a scent most heavenly—
Ambrosia of the gods it seems, my humming bird!
I see you streak toward one bloom—but wait! A word
Of caution! Do you not see those thick and flanking pairs of leaf-like horns,
Their edges bristling thick with black and hook-like thorns?
I know you're swift and confident, but do you dare
To dart within that bloom and brave the unknown danger there?
Alas, you do! That heavenly scent of nectar draws you in,
Those fleshy leaves close quickly and their black hooks pierce your skin.

That bloom exudes digestive juices as I hear your last shrill chitter.
'Tis sad your fickle flitterings have led you to a doom so bitter.
Yet on the bright side we should look, for following your final squeal
A gorgeous flower blooms with joy as it digests its sumptuous meal.

Dr. Cat Tree

Jessica Amanda Salmonson

Dr. Cat Tree
    killed an old geezer;
Sawed off his head,
    kept it in her freezer.

"Why did you do it,
    Dr. Cat Tree?
Why is he dead;
    can you inform me?"

"I needed meat,
    I needed it quick;
Had to eat brains
    or I'd've been sick."

Dr. Cat Tree,
    the grim physician:
Doing harm is
    her principal mission.

Hide at the pig farm,
    hide in a hole;
Avoid Dr. Tree—
    She has no soul.

The Nightmares

Wade German

Trois spectres familiers hantent mes heures sombres.
—Leconte de Lisle, "Les Spectres"

I.

Three Nightmares haunt the ruins of my mind
Like revenants that every night return
With bright red terrors, wicked and refined.

At first they followed in my dreams, then turned
To follow me across the wall of sleep—
A strange, invasive species, I would learn

On waking from a dark, abyssal deep
Of dreams to find them gathered in my room
Like awful toys an evil child might keep.

In every corner now, their shadows loom;
At every step I take they're close behind
With awful whisperings, weird taunts of doom . . .

Three Nightmares haunt the remnants of my mind.

II.

In Sleep's dimension, there are stranger things
That rise unreal to live, then dissipate
Like phantoms vanishing on vapour wings.

These Nightmare-things my mind did not create.
They show me dead horizons, seas of gore;
The visions swiftly change, but won't abate.

It is as if my mind were some grimoire
In which the Nightmares scribble evil spells
To conjure images of death and war,

To summon baleful clangors from black bells
That seem a demon choir, as it sings
With iron tongues to praise the outer hells . . .

In Sleep's black mansion there are stranger things . . .

III.

I see the shadows of those things unseen,
These evil visitors that feed my sight
With landscapes most unhallowed and unclean.

A spectral form of psychic parasite,
They burrowed through the doors that are my dreams—
If dreams are barrows, they are barrow-wights,

With eerie voices screeching quiet screams . . .
I do not understand the awful sounds,
Though all these visions speak to me, it seems.

Is it, perhaps, my mind has run aground
On reefs of madness, wrecked on shores of spleen . . . ?
Like leeches to my soul forever bound,

I sense the shadows of three things unseen—!

IV.

The colours of these terrors slowly change;
In total darkness, one can clearly see
Pale horrors for dark glories, wondrous, strange . . .

The sky, a slab of jet-black masonry,
I've slid across my roof to seal my tomb.
The Nightmares, tittering so close to me,

Still send me visions through the cloistered gloom,
Gifting me with a true sight to affirm
A truth that only sane minds may exhume:

The world is but an open grave, it squirms . . .
I see it and withdraw, a man estranged,
For those who walk upon the earth are worms . . .

The substance of my nightmares—it has changed . . .

The Voice of the *Mary Celeste*

M. F. Webb

'Tis on these broken nights I hear it most,
A keening wind as through a splintered mast.
Then melody unnerves the shrouded coast

As if a thousand troubadours were cast
To sing and play their lutes along the shore.
I lie awake and listening, aghast,

Until I cannot bear the cry and roar
And fly outside, resolved to know what sound
So rudely disconcerts my very core,

But never see a ship or boat aground,
Not sea lions distressed or lowing whale,
Nor evidence of living creature drowned—

Save one elusive flourish far and pale,
As if a cloud were fashioned from a sail.

A Longer Winter

Benjamin Blake

Everything is washed out;
Stark trees with branches bare.
Light is weak,
And little warmth can be found
In the porcelain arms
of ghosts.

Feeble bones,
Chilled to the touch;
Left behind to fend for myself,
Crazed and half-starved,
With only a curved dagger
For company.

The snow-covered corpses
Have become nonchalant mile markers,
Barely remembered along the way.
A man can become conditioned to kill,
With little effort at all
On anyone's part.

Succubus Waltz

Joshua Gage

This tomb that time forgot
swells foul with mold and bone.
An acrid stench of rot
exudes from every stone.

The candles that I've lit
dance shadows round the room.
I slice my fingertip
to paint unholy runes.

She lulls me to her breast
with a hand as soft as sin,
then pulls me through the steps.
So our waltz begins.

Her body undulates
in naked confidence.
The catafalque awaits
a different type of dance.

A Witch's Memoir

Ashley Dioses

Harold

My name was Harold—Alfred, possibly—
A nobleman was I, or . . . royalty?
My memories are lacking clarity—
For since my death, they've held no loyalty.

The power I once held must have been great—
So great, I darkly let myself succumb.
My wife, my ball and chain, was just a weight,
And yet she showed me what I would become. . . .

The Curse

"Twist the bird's neck and make him see the past,
  Then cross the eyes and blind him to his path.
  Now cross its legs to misdirect, at last,
  And for six generations, bear my wrath!"

Romani were they, or perhaps Santera,
  Who spoke this curse upon the rotten chicken,
  And put a sudden end to my grand era?
  Upon my cryptic death, my soul did sicken. . . .

The Battle

I could not face my end without a war!
I tried reversing it, for I was Gifted,
But how I failed!—it ripped right through my core,
And to Oblivion I fell, and drifted.

Awakening within a life unknown
Did not mean shedding my horrific past.
No, I had not come to this age alone—
For through the portal my past love was cast.

The Lover

I quite ignored her, yet she still loved me.
Her longing grew into a force unseen.
In ghostly chains, no longer was I free—
She clung to me, to be my only queen.

She does not know that she is dead and seeks
To be my only love, yet I no longer
Remember her, and even when she speaks
To me, my love for her grows never stronger.

The Punishment

Once generously Gifted, I am weak.
Once loved so selflessly, I am neglected.
Once powerful and strong, I am now meek.
Once blessed so blissfully, I am infected.

I don't know who I was or what I did—
It does not matter much, for my soul knows.
My punishment is that I can't get rid
Of this old curse—we all reap what we sow.

A Frenzy of Witches

David Barker

When the witches had enough
Of eating children on the bluff,
They descended to the village,
There to further kill and pillage—
Slashing throats and bashing heads,
Torching clergy in their beds,
Casting spells on all they hated,
Till their violent lusts were sated.

Done, they fell upon their knees,
Each as pious as you please;
Begged absolution from the Goat,
Who cloaked each crone in his black coat.
All returned then to the hills,
Boasting of their arcane thrills.

The Girl and Her Wolf Dog

Christina Sng

I follow your tracks to the deserted road;
They lead me to the deep forest.
This is where we loved to roam,
In a time not too long ago.

Your paw prints end near the broken cabin
And behind, there, your bones.
I pull out my scythe from its tattered sheath
And enter the killer's home.

Here he sits, surrounded by bottles,
Your collar around his wrist.
In a single blow, I cut off his arm
And catch your collar in my fist.

He pulls out his gun and I sever that arm
And stab him till he is finally dead.
I gather your bones into my arms
And breathe life back into them.

Slowly your flesh knits, layer by layer
Till you are good and whole again.
I return you your collar and hold you close
As you deeply inhale and lick my nose.

I kiss each head and whistle your name
With our common refrain,
"Come, Cerberus,
It is time to go home."

The Vortex That Ate Poseidonis

Manuel Pérez-Campos

I.

Out of the depths of the dreamlands it came,
a phantasmal fringe that breach'd the buttresses
of the city-wide wall, its fathomless
turbulence that of incipient flame.
It separated architrave from dome
and the larghetto of the aqueduct
from the amaranth-cultivated hill.
It disassembl'd the spectrum of marble
and rose and render'd Mt. Zos amok,
forcing out of its fissures igniform loam
until its cliff-balanc'd pharos seem'd small.
Peplum-clad youths of decadent conduct
fled in electrum chariots, but muck
and soot pour'd from above, sapping their will.

II.

The temple's idol of Stheno, palladium
of its necromancies, vanish'd upward;
and half a world away, a torch-steer'd trireme
became engulf'd in an abrupt tentacle.
A new immeasurable gloaming
forc'd its saffron on daedal balconies.
Flesh-wilting orchids detach'd the queen's head
and fizz'd until her argent lips kept foaming.
A griffin, releas'd, soar'd out with eldritch scream.
Tier'd villas unravell'd, forming a graveyard;
eunuchs, who had thought their lives infrangible,
wept: 'Twas thus that the many-tower'd ease
of that isle which darken'd a millennium
tumbl'd into the abode of the dead.

To the memory of Clark Ashton Smith

Fleeting Existence

J. T. Edwards

Lost on the sea of forgotten days
Wandering aimlessly through grey placid halls
Memories morph into cold uncaring shadows
Alone and paralyzed on the precipice of forever
Suddenly hurtling through nightmare oblivion
Flung into the warm maw of death

Terrarium

Oliver Smith

Vengeance followed through the winter;
A man followed through the snow.
A trail led over the frozen water
And following he found
    A paradise enclosed: bottle garden and glasshouse sky
    Where the yellow waters of a river flowed

    Between cloud topped pillars of greening bronze

And the trunks of trees grown mountain-high.
Unearthly petals sang a song so honey sweet
That golden nectar fell like sun and rain
On green boughs;
    Ripe fruits burst their swollen guts and gushed

    Slime and seed with the malevolent fertility
    Of a Hell unvanquished in primordial Eden.

Above a swarm of bright beetles feasted on
The enemy he sought, who hung like a purple plum:
Vine-wrapped among the jungle leaves,
While below

    Where lush thickets knotted branch and root
    A hundred gardeners lay among the stranglers:
    Their skulls grinned a white-toothed welcome.

The Return

Ian Futter

The mocking masks
lie grinning on the shore,
amongst the severed heads of serpents
who will tempt no more.

The coal-black waters
hide the darkest star,
whose base and blank reflection
rakes the surface like a scar.

The ticking clocks
all fold their final tocks
amongst the crippled corpses
that lie screaming on the rocks.

Through rotten roots
and broken boughs, I come:
A weary, wan, consumptive shade,
expelled from heaven's slum,

To place my final face
amidst the grins,
where spiders peep through wet, webbed holes
through which my vision dimmed.

For far beneath the lake
a foulness sings
and beckons me toward the depths,
away from fickle things.

Gas Giant

F. J. Bergmann

The shuttle's wake slices
through a buzzing swarm
of something nasty that splats
the hull in a way that does not
tempt us to be inquisitive.
Hierarchically, they aren't
what we have to worry about—
the dominant life-forms
are lower in the atmosphere.
Our pilot finesses our descent,
palm on control-pad, sinking
past pale, amorphous clouds
of methane ice. Turbines
whine against resistance
as the gales grow denser.
Thicker strata hide hirsute,
scorpion-like monsters, but
they are at a disadvantage
when matched with those
swimming further down.
We keep on falling, canary
looking for a black cat
hiding in a coal mine.

Our AI validates the signal
we home in on, emissaries
to whatever apex predator
dwells at the base of an upside-
down evolutionary pinnacle
poised in the heavy hells
below. We don't know what
we'll find; don't know what
we'll say. All we know
is that it believes
it is dreaming *us*.

The Spirit of the Place

Liam Garriock

The earth is ancient. The snow-capped mountains and the humid forests and the deep seas are ancient, as are the billions of stars in the night sky. Animals of all shapes and sizes have prowled and crawled through the barren plains and the mossy woods and soared through the clear blue skies, and humans have erected their homes on the primeval land, have begun fires to illuminate the hostile dark, and have told one another marvellous stories. These tales, passed down from generation to generation as oral blood, have their origins in the landscape and are embedded in them like phantom jewels hidden behind mouldering walls. The landscape becomes a vast and varied conduit battery through which the psychic energy of the stories is channelled by receptive, visionary minds. These visitors, wandering artists and poets, shamans and seers who have inherited the mystic wisdom of Paul Nash and Blake, are pilgrims in search of the numinous, and they are drawn to these sacred sites by the occult energies that they emit, then they excavate the soil and the stone for the recondite powers so that they may share it with the penurious world. For them, every standing stone, every hill, every Roman remain, every tree, is a receptacle that stores unimaginable, primordial power within its core. And this power is not confined to ancient places: all cities, regardless of age, are built atop ancient soil with a deep past, and the capricious pagan powers buried therein travel into the glass and concrete and stone like sentient electricity. When these powers reach a climax, timeless tales of love and joy and bitterness and cruelty are re-enacted, like some metaphysical trap set in motion by fate. And these shocking cosmic outbreaks of bygone violence and enchantment are recorded in the pages of the book of history, read and turned by an unknowable divinity. And while the city grows and nurtures its own myths, the old ways continue to pervade the wild countryside, where the elder languages are spoken, and where men and women still see the faeries in their hidden courts in the hills. Here, the ghosts of ancient kings ride across the desolate land on spectral steeds, and votive offerings are left for the older gods. Our world is a haunted world blessed with wonderful magic and cursed with terrible enchantments, and its spells linger on even after the cities are empty and full of dust. Men and women and children have forgotten their roots, and their connection to the land has been severed by the encroaching forces of modernity; but the heathen gods and ancient spirits linger on in the hills and the rivers and the trees, worshipped and feared by those who still remember the old ways. Incantatory songs and poems are uttered from their wizened throats, songs and poems of magic and enduring strengths. No matter what cataclysm sweeps the earth, whether it be tsunami or atomic war, the spirits of the landscape persist and dance on the solemn and lonely moors.

Red

Mary Krawczak Wilson

She took her tea past two
In the garden by the pond
Where the swallows soared on
Trees tainted in a red hue.

At first, it was a small speck—
A red drop that dribbled down
Upon her translucent gown
Too soft and slight to detect.

Suddenly it soaked the ground,
Blanketing the pond in red.
She watched as the waters bled
In the earth without a sound.

Beyond the pond scum and mud,
It broke its borders in slow motion
Drowning her in its own ocean
Of evil and blasphemous blood.

The Old Courthouse

Don Webb

As you drive into famous Lockhart on 183,
Pass the five BBQ restaurants (including "oldest in Texas"),
You'll see a glorious three story red and white new courthouse
True "Hill Country" 1880s splendor.
You might miss the old courthouse,
A dingy yellow brick building across from a cotton gin.
Its sad faded sign says "And Museum."
Inside are the old gaol and the old gallows.
If you're a morbid sort you can climb the platform
The one window is aligned with the old clocktower
So each prisoner could look upon human time
One last time before his neck snapped.
The old warden thought it poetic.
With the irony that attends such things,
The clock itself stopped during the Reagan administration.
I like to watch the tourists with their stupid selfies
And their HOOK'EM HORNS! T-shirts
Every now and then I'll see one
Whose heart stops
Whose soul Awakens for a second
Who swallows hard feeling the noose that once hung there.
Like Odhinn, they glimpse the Runes
They don't shoot a selfie.
They leave quietly and sit in their Nissans and Kia Souls
A moment, before driving back
on life's highway,
And looking for a Dairy Queen.

The Black Hunt

Adam Bolivar

On Hallowe'en a hunter rides
    With hounds as black as coal;
And like a fox who slinks and hides,
    His quarry is a soul,

Which flickers like a lanthorn's light
    Deep in Yᵉ Yellow'd Reed;
You'll see it in the moonless night
    And mimicked in a swede.

'Tis Jack for whom the dark man hunts,
    This rider all in black,
For there is none who so affronts
    The Devil as spry Jack,

For once Jack kissed the Devil's wife,
    Pale Lilith's crimson lips,
And then I swear upon my life,
    He slipped between her hips—

So now Jack flees the rider's wrath
    And hides deep in Yᵉ Reed,
For like a hare he knows the path
    To shun the hounds with speed.

And there he waits until the light,
    When dawns All Hallow's Day;
The hunter then will take his flight,
    The hounds will fade away.

Forever the Covens Break Us

Claire Smith

Our country's broken to pieces . . .
Cackles tell us the witches stalk
The coven all in uniform:
Pointed hats, black capes,
Broomsticks

Like ravens perched on steel rods,
They carry red laser guns
Across their backs.
Robotic cats yowl.
We're driven down,

Below the ground
To hide in reinforced
Concrete bunkers. We huddle
In fear, horror, while witches
Conjure green-gas monsters

To work for them—
Tentacles stretched round
The sewerage system;
Hunched bodies climb
The drains' ladders

Tongues release spit;
Turn victims to stone . . .

The king's men try to save us—
Duck captured witches
Head first into water-tanks.
But the real hags escape,
While poor innocents
Drown without ceremony.
The real witches always return
Come back twice as strong.

When dusk falls
On skyscrapers,
On apartment blocks,
And shopping malls,
They soar high

Gathered in airships,
To drop bombs,
Rip our city to bits.
We only dream of peace—
An end to the daily onslaughts

Daylight hours bring the shock
Of the damage done.
We try to escape the borders
Forced to scatter, and run,
Driven all over, far and wide.

Lycanthrope Moon

Frank Coffman

The full moon scuds through ghost-grey winter clouds;
The stars peek through the racing gaps between.
The cottages are locked and shuttered tight,
For horror's shape by moonlight might be seen.

Each cycle of the moon brings nights of dread,
As gibbous waxing heads toward the full.
And memories of the ones long lost refresh,
And very clear are those of recent cull.

Crosses are kept on every homestead wall,
And candles are alight in every room.
Each threshold holds a sprig of mistletoe,
And wolfsbane flowers in bright blue-purple bloom
Around each locked and fastened window pane.
Within, the villagers in fear and care prepare
With keen-edged iron, poignards silver tipped,
And torches—lest a monster enter there.

Some months, a small group of the very brave
Go forth by night to seek the monstrous track
And kill the man-wolf curse that haunts their woods.
But only rarely any man comes back.

Those few that have have either killed a beast,
Watched it turn back into someone they know,

Or they alone escaped. Some bitten by the thing
Are put to death before the change can show.

The folk knew long ago no single man,
Over the years, had been their monthly plight.
Somehow, the heirs of a long-dead patriarch
Had howled and hunted the moon-blighted night.

By daylight on the morn after the moon,
They venture forth to see if there are dead.
A better fate to die from claw and fang
Than to be welcomed to that clan of dread.

And any of their folk who end up missing
Are reckoned to be lost and are estranged.
Some few, who've ventured back after those nights,
Are caged one month, until they've either changed
Or proved themselves still men and only men;
The ones who change are quickly killed and burned.
The townsfolk revel at such ghastly blazes—
But blame them not—for they have awfully learned.

And so, the people of that region live
To keep the phases of the orb in view,
Knowing that, at the full, the moon will bring
Horrors that are, for them, both old and new.

Look Beyond

Darrell Schweitzer

When first you gaze into the sorcerer's glass
you see only yourself, a reflection:
the innocent or fool or wise one,
eyes wide with expectation or terror,
face unlined or deeply scarred.
The details don't matter.
Look beyond.
Now the wondrous realms appear,
the crystalline mountains, the forests and fields made all of light,
the dark towers on lonely hilltops,
the wide, gleaming rivers that drift off to nowhere
beneath a brilliant moon, over the edge of the world,
into space and stars and dreams.
Look beyond.

The monsters rear up, ravening with delight
at the destruction of worlds, their gaze
locked with yours as if in a hideous dance.
This too will pass. It is vanity, a trivial game
of curses and dreadful runes.
Look beyond,
into the real abyss, the all-devouring void
without magic or gods,
the utter annihilation of morality and volition.
Look at the shadow cast by nothing.
This is where it begins, this is
the first step of your pilgrimage.

Pumpkin, Oh Pumpkin!

Will Hart

(*For K. A. Opperman's Thirtieth Birthday*)

You were growing fine
Upon the vine,
But now you've been cut off.

You may not have bled,
But you'll soon be dead,
As Kyle, The Pumpkin King,
Digs in you like a trough.

He'll take his knife to your firm skin
And carve for you a face,
Where light will shine
From your vacant rind,
And you'll rot in your public place.

So enjoy your final days,
Waiting for the carver's knife,
Knowing you were born for this—
A Jack O' Lantern's Life.

The World Turns

Kendall Evans

The game goes on . . .
The World Turns
With unfathomable
Precision;
The other card holders
Make decisions:
Call or raise,
Hold or fold.
Though poker faces
surround me,
I am grounded
In thee;
The table spins—
The cards are dealt,
The fates are cast,
Emotions quelled,
Players say: "Hit me—
Hit me again."
Masochistic requests,
Temptations beyond redemption;
The cosmos swirls,
Chaos unfolds,

The table turns
Like a merry-go-round;
And do they know
That the cards I hold
Are from
Some other world?

Looking After Death

John Reinhart

I lost myself
as illumined clouds embalmed my soul,
so now I'll take what I can get.

The naysayers, doomchanters
have yet to decant death where
I lost myself,

gaining everything I have now.
Souls are the hardest to come by,
so I'll take what I can get,

even if it's dog—a last resort—
a man's got to eat.
I lost myself

to a simple gamble at the crossroads,
ready now to join the hunt
where I'll take what I can get.

A little less core strength, a lot more hunger,
I walked that labyrinth,
I lost myself—
now I'll take what I can get.

The King of Horrors, Howard Phillips Lovecraft

Charles Lovecraft

Start Chant: The King

Quintessence of a mind the dreams that were,
And which race still in that jewelled skull, till age
Itself dissolves, and in his black-eyed stare
An entourage of fears proclaims a sage.

Thus jungles full of paralysing fright,
With haunted visions, twisted scenes he knew,
Are in the horrors always found by night
As the key nourishment that his soul drew.

The Shadow out of Time

Five years a stranger's face the mirror locked
Upon shrewd eyes, and dark things stirred the self.
Invading mind chilled deeply as it mocked.
At last his memory regained its health.
Beneath the deserts of an austral land,
Mid fallen columns, dusts that swirl between,
The willing fool would find *in his own hand*
The writing from the ages he had been!

The Unnamable

Upon the next night there arose in dark,
From long-hushed aisles of tombs where forces free,
A thing that lay on heart its monstrous mark
And cataclysm of what should not be.

Some window panes bear traces of the dead,
Repellent visages that sear the soul.
When those dark forces come to life we dread,
Or worse—we end up chewed and gouged for role.

The Book

Upon the third night I knew rest had gone,
With shaking jewels of beaded sweat that burned
Upon my beetling brow a wedged thorn crown,
And foul, dark meaning of the runes I learned.

I tried to send the book away, but found
That it returned by black uncanny means.
I was to that thing tied and moored and bound,
Through what ill-fated climes and dark demesnes.

The Dunwich Horror

When Wilbur Whateley died he was half-god,
Seed-crossed with monstrous godhead from the blue,
And in his steps a dark divinity trod.
In Dunwich his twin-brother spread and grew.

That thing got loose and tore the woods apart;
The evil flowed from earth's repugnant maw.
I still see now the trees bent to their heart;
Occultist powders last revealed the awe.

End Chant: Father Lovecraft, Sleep No More

L guides through metaphysic mists that thin,
Revealing callipers of other times;
The circles and dimensions that da Vin-
Ci sings meet in the gong of St. Toad's chimes.

Thus strained by sleeplessness for all drugs' worth,
The wilderness of aeons onward wings;
While from the cosmic planes beyond the earth
The rapture of weird destinies he brings!

The Scrying Mirror

Chelsea Arrington

When ships upon menacing rocks are thrown
And the moon's a sickle in the ebony sky;
When ravens sing out a threatening tone,
My lord calls out in a terrible cry.

My name he invokes by oaths infernal;
By demons of flame and wind and sea.
A madman possessed by gods nocturnal,
He beckons by powers three times three.

From shadowy realms of darkness and shade
I appear to work my master's will.
Augur and magic are my lord's trade;
Malicious and loathsome is his skill.

He speaks in riddles, his eyes fire-red,
Demanding portents and hideous sooth.
Malignant black spells within him are bred,
Laying waste to the sweetness of beauty and youth.

Impressions of serpents and coins conjure I;
Doomed lovers, kings poisoned, drowned ships, and roads bleak.
Before him, the spiced lands of Araby lie;
Fell secrets of future and past do I speak.

When death and carnage enough has he seen;
When my warnings at last have been plaintively sung,
His skin sparkles with an unholy sheen
And a velvet cloth over me now is hung.

I am his servant, the black mirror's slave,
Forever consigned to immortal doom.
Slumber and dream in a living grave:
The wizard's dark agent, seer in gloom.

Desert Witch

Rob Matheny

Desert witch, desert witch,
Where have you been?
Cavorting with demons?
Committing blasphemous sin?

Desert witch, desert witch,
What evils you speak!
What lies you tell!
What slander you shriek!

Desert witch, desert witch,
Do you dream at night?
I wonder what spectacles
Fill you with fright.

Desert witch, desert witch,
Please cast your spell.
Tell me the future,
What can you foretell?

Desert witch, desert witch,
Give me a treat!
Some candy, so tasty,
Toothsome and sweet!

Desert witch, desert witch,
You're so evil it's true,

Even the devil
Has doubts about you!

Desert witch, desert witch,
Is that blood on your hands?
Why are you smiling?
I don't quite understand.

Desert witch, desert witch,
Witch of the sand!
Enshroud me with blindness,
Give me your hand!

Desert witch, desert witch,
I'm sinking below!
My life is escaping!
Don't let me go!

Desert witch, desert witch,
Now the truth becomes clear:
You feed on malevolence,
Madness, and fear!

Desert witch, desert witch,
Accursed is your name,
And yet I still find
That I love you the same.

The Milk Hare

David Barker

A dancing witch I spy beneath the moon,
In gauzy gown that slips from shoulders bare.
While singing verses unadorned by tune,
Her shrill voice resonates the silvered air.
Entranced, I follow her into the weald
And thicket deep where she prepares the hare
Who does her bidding when the pact is sealed,
So that the dame may take of milk her share.

A rabbit formed of sticks and drops of blood,
The beldame's kiss arouses it to life.
She gives her oath that it will suck the cow,
Yet morning finds me lying in the mud,
A fool for having followed this false wife;
Bereft of milk, the witch I disavow.

The Fetch

K. A. Opperman

Halloween is drawing nearer;
Pumpkin lamps at twilight glow,
And the attic's antique mirror,
Dim with dust, begins to show
Her angelic face the clearer
As the autumn nights grow drearer,
And her face to me is dearer,
Dearer than I even know.

Halloween is soon returning;
Witches haunt the night unseen,
And my heart and soul are yearning
For the glamored eyes of green
Of the lass I am discerning
In the mirror clearer turning—
Love or devil, I'll be learning
On the night of Halloween.

Nosferatu

David Schembri

Shadows drape my mind of late
As I walk through tainted lands;
'Tis my absent, demon state,
Forcing out my shaking hands.

How I gaze at crimson skies,
Raised through darkness, far from home,
Vultures fret around my cries;
Now I mourn: "I am alone!"

Smells, they find me—oh so sweet;
Hunger travels to my head,
Takes me now to thy warm treat,
Luscious drink of blooming red!

Underneath a veil of flesh,
Pulsing, pumping, from the bed,
I now drink, my purpose fresh,
I now drink till you are dead.

Hiding the Corpse

Shawn Ramsey

The man we killed had vacant eyes,
Soft and dumb with incognition.
At the river they apprised
Neither hate nor recognition.

The Pearl that was one eye still shines
In the Hudson River bottom;
Its murk is thick and it prevents
The face reciting its designs.

The ledger of the cruel and just
Lay shut down where his blood congealed,
Among the clam beds and the rust.
They keep the Secret Name concealed.

Down where the currents take and give
Turn the negotiations of misrule,
Where titanthropic beasts relive
Extinctions instantaneous and cruel.

Predations of the curious
Must dare the aquatic for reprise.
Our rationales mysterious,
The waters keep our alibis.

The Final Masquerade

Alan Gullette

I.

Outside the tall and castellated walls
Of the old abbey stood the final guest
Of the King in Yellow's masquerade ball.

Above, a rift in solemn clouds revealed
A glimpse of star-points far away—and near,
The welcome light of torches burned aloft.

Within, the revelries were underway:
Masked dancers danced by particolored light,
Music and wicked laughter filled the night.

Camilla dressed as Mercury was there;
She moved across the room on wingèd feet
Past Prospero, Miranda, and Ariel.

Cassilda was dressed as a Spanish saint
Who blasphemed and swore obscenities
At Cardinal Richelieu and his retinue.

The King himself was like the Devil dressed,
With horns, red cape, and pointed tail,
A bearded, pallid mask with eyes of glass.

II.

Into the mass of costumed revelers—
Who shrink away at once to let him pass—
Strides boldly forth the late-arriving guest.

The music stops, all merriment is paused;
The other guests all gasp, or hiss, or scoff
As at some crudity—or blasphemy.

For the strange guest in golden silk was dressed,
Refined though cut in scalloped tatters,
His face obscured by a yellow mask:

He wore the habit of the King in Yellow!
Yet all knew that the King's guise was the Devil,
So who was this crude and fearless fellow?

Straight to the Devil strode this yellow king.
"Who might the Host of this regal fête be?" he asked.
"To judge by your habit, it might be thee!" the answer.

Although he tried to speak with courtly tongue,
The visitor's accent was a country one,
Which also would explain his boorish manner.

III.

"Perhaps if we set our disguises aside
  We'll see each other as we truly are,"
  The Devil proffered and doffed his pallid mask—

  Only to reveal his daily silken mask,
  Identical to the visitor's disguise.
  "Now I know who *you* are," said the guest,

"Although you still are masked, mine Host"—
  With a bow. "And also you know *me*, sir,
  Though likewise I am still masked," he avowed.

  By now his country twang was plainly heard.
  "That *I* know *you*? I hardly think so, sir!"
  The true King laughed, but sounded ill-at-ease.

"How can we know? Remove your own disguise!"
  "I tell you still, you know my name!" as he unmasked.
  "Why, Alasper!" cried the King before he stopped . . .

  And having named the guest unknown to all
  But him, the King unmasked himself as well,
  As being familiar with this country man.

IV.

"Indeed, my name is Alasper," he said;
"Indeed, I was your countryman—and friend!
We herded goats to the mountain pastures

And made burnt offerings to Hastur—"
At once the King denied the stranger's claim
And looked with desperate eyes to his old friends;

But none there was who would be fooled anew.
The boldness of the claimant and his claim
Usurped at once the false King from their minds.

"I suppose you told them of Lake Hali?"
The intruder smirked, continuing
His diminution of the King . . .

"When you began to call yourself a god,
Or god-king from the stars—the Hyades—
'Carcosa with its towers behind the moon!'—

"We laughed you out of town, your madness known . . .
I see you have done better in the city
Convincing others of your outré fancy!"

V.

The King in Yellow raised a hand to strike
The interloper with the grinning face—
But all the others turned their smiles on *him*.

And so the stage was set for him to speak—
To justify, perchance explain himself
To the minions of his dubious estate.

"Indeed, I came here from the countryside.
Indeed, I was a lowly shepherd born;
But I have risen above mere mountains!

"One day, I wearied of my daily chores;
I left the valley, climbed the highest ridge
And found the mountain pool they call Lake Hali.

"I sat to rest and stared into the pool
Whose shifting surface masked the cloudy depths,
But as the breeze died, it grew strangely calm.

"At once I overcame a baseless fear:
Into the darkest depths I peered and peered
But there was only blackness without end . . .

VI.

"I did not sense the length of time that passed—
 The holy waters smooth as darkling glass—
 When I beheld two shining stars descend:

"Twin suns that slid from a field of stars!
 As I knelt, face to face with the dark,
 I saw my face had turn an ashen gray.

"Trembling there with horror and despair
 My visage frozen in a frightful grimace!
 So, masking myself, I fled the place, the scene—

"The petty people with their petty gods—
 And gave myself over to a nameless fate,
 The truth I felt beside the mountain lake . . .

"With eyes that see in darkness, beyond bounds—
 No near or far—I see behind the moon!
 That night, I flew down from the stars!

"And seizing the moment, I seized the throne,
 Tossed into the tumult of history—
 A Caesar of the moment—my will is done!"

VII.

"The truth you found was not profound, but shallow,"
  The country fellow said, wise past his years.
"In failing to find your soul, you lost it!

"For the fear of death is in everyone,
  But the fear of living life as a no-one
  Became for you an evil curse—or worse!

"The twin stars you saw fall from the skies
  Were nothing but your own reflected eyes
  In the lake—an error of perspective!

"You identify with God, but only
  God the Destroyer: you cannot create.
  This 'living god' you impersonate is a delusion of grandeur!"

The guests all shed their masks and shed their fears.
  With newfound freedom they deposed the king
  And sent him back to his mountain region.

And so it came to pass that the King in Yellow
  Was just an ordinary fellow—
  His claimed nobility a grand illusion!

A Modern Exorcism

Ian Futter

"How squeamish are you?"
he asked.
I asked why.
He said,
"I just need to wind this screw
into your eye."

"On this side; in the Canthus,
for my skill is well known,
where smell-sense
meets your vision,
I will twist the thing home."

"Will it hurt?"
I enquired.
"Will the visions then cease?"
"Oh, yes,"
he replied.
"I will bring your release."

So I stifled my screams,
as he ground through the
bone.
And the demons all
fled.

Now I'm free,

but alone.

Winter 2018

The Vellum of the Damned

Joshua Gage

We hunch in our scriptorium
    to meet our masters' dark demands.
With shoulders hunched by candlelight
we labor through the snowy night
and copy down unholy rites
    across the vellum of the damned.

Our acolytes slave through the day
    to craft materials by hand.
They work to keep our inkwells filled
with blood from sacrifices killed.
With raven feathers for our quills
    we scribe the vellum of the damned.

Some bastard's mother has been paid
to offer up her suckling babe,
and now the whetstone hones the blade
    to gather the vellum of the damned.

Berserker

Benjamin Blake

Throwing axes cut the evening air,
As storm clouds roll in overhead.
Wipe the blood from chapped lips
And take solace in
The sound of breaking bones.

The rain now falls
On these mounds of blackened flesh.
Bodies stretched for miles
That shall never see a proper tomb
And died for an unseen king.

I cut the heart out from the chest
And consumed it where I knelt.
The crows were already on wing,
Keen beaks sharpened on graveyard stone.

Thunder tears asunder
The vault of the heavens
Over this unholy mass,
These killing fields,
That I call home.

When We Fall

Christina Sng

Just another
Supermarket run
With my favorite ones,
Pushing a full trolley,
Baby in my arms.

When the zombies strike
As they inevitably do,
I pull down
The graffitied metal grilles,
Protecting us few.

We have us
A plumber,
A gardener,
A doctor,
An engineer too.

The supplies
And the roof garden
Will keep us alive
Till soon
The heat and humidity

Melt the undead
Then we take up arms
Against our true enemies,
The looters and the gangs.
Thank goodness we

Have an armory too.

Mama Drool

Ross Balcom

o towering witch

casting
an infinite shadow

on my bedroom
floor

drooling madwoman

mama drool
mama drool

dissolve me
in your saliva

mama drool
mama drool

terminal
liquefaction

my one desire

dissolve
my flesh and bones

liquefy me
utterly

let me be lost
in your witch-whirl

forever

o mama
mama drool

Germina Amoris

Oliver Smith

He followed a song among mold-mottled ferns
Under gilded vegetation grown in wide umbrellas
Sheltering paths from the interminable drip

Of condensation;
  Where jaguar and serpent slept beneath the dome
  And an artificial sun illuminated
  A shrine where a perfect statue stood, an idol

Among palms that curved in a titan's bower.
He found a sentient lotus dreaming all desires:

A goddess surrounded with the stench of dying flowers
She sat
  Belly-fruit grimly, grossly lush and overripe
  Limbs orchid-mottled, engorged with sorcery
  Lips smiling in parody of convolvulus and lily;

Come dance among the jungle darkness among the leaves,
Come dance among the thousand rippling streams.

She led him through sweet flowering branches
To a verdant bed
  Where she held him in her languid roots;
  His body flowered in the ecstasy of her embrace
  Her curious tendrils burrowing through his tender flesh.

The Ballad of 3 A.M.

M. F. Webb

Hour upon hour the night birds are sweeping
The stars from the sky with ineffable wings.
Burnt like a candle, her vigil I'm keeping,
A fragility brimming with breakable things.

Minute on minute, the darkness is ringing
A clamorous bell in a tenebrous clock
And memories fixed in formation go winging
A mad murmuration, a shadowy flock.

Hollow and hulled, as the night birds are stalking
The indigent moon to some farther abyss,
I build of my heartache a cradle for rocking,
As if I could conjure her back with a wish.

Hidden as dawn is the face I was kissing,
Lost as the hours once devoured by sleep;
An uncharted sky and a moon that's gone missing,
No scintillant smile on the face of the deep.

Hour upon hour, as the night birds are sweeping
The stars from the sky with ineffable wings,
Burnt like a candle, her vigil I'm keeping,
A fragility brimming with breakable things.

Past, Present, and Future

Liam Garriock

The past is a romanticised corpse in danger of being used as propaganda for a thing that never was and never will be. Rolling pastures and frolicking fauns and shimmering lakes—these are mere inventions created by dead writers and nostalgic poets. The true visionary envisions not the past but the future; the past to him or her is a psychic graveyard whence warnings and wisdoms are taken. The future, however, is a garden that must be tended to so that beautiful flowers may bloom, otherwise time risks repeating itself. The goal is not to resurrect a long-lost golden age from the ashes and mists of Time, but to create a lasting golden age for the future.

You are trapped in the stillborn present, a spectral parenthesis hanging in a void where the past slowly dies and the future is inexorably conceived. The sky, the birds, the stones, the trees, everything here is a hollow ghost awaiting personal death and cosmic apocalypse. The sun madly burns in the blue and cloudy sky, and the winds blow through the bushes and the trees. You are wise, for arcane sources have imparted to you the truth surrounding this precarious phantom world. Yes, madness and evil run through the heart of the world, swimming in its tempestuous seas and vein-like sewers. A dead leaf rolling along the grass in the wind contains unknown consciousness. Those people whom you once liked and knew, they are vampires tugging at your heart, and those buildings you loved are prisons masking corruption and deceit. The churches are beautiful, sombre stone goddesses with ugly, lying hearts. The worst kind of traitor is one's own self. Can you be sure that you know what you want? Ask yourself: what is the ultimate reality of the world? Joy or despair, life or death, substance or shade? Will you ever know the answer, if there is any answer?

Odd Todd

Jessica Amanda Salmonson

Odd Todd, fanged and clawed,
Crawled out from the Land of Nod.
You don't want to meet him
He's too much like God
A psychotic cretin
A terrible fraud.

He pissed the rivers
He farted the skies
He vomited terrors
From out of his eyes.

The moon is his forehead
The sun is his ass
That shines like a mandrill's behind
In blue, orange, and red
A cancerous mass
That makes us all wish we were blind.

The Waning Hours of Woe

J. T. Edwards

Dead gleaming eyes in a cloudless sky
The moon bathes the empty streets in golden gloom
Demonic cries echo from the eldritch woods
Mournful villagers gather by dwindling fires of grief
Longing for those haunting chimes at midnight
When sorrow sings for the final time

Sea Creatures

Mary Krawczak Wilson

The sea was once a luminous mirror
That reflected a life without pain or fear;
Its waters were cool, blue, and calm,
And its fish and fowl thrived without qualms.

But one day the skies were striated in gray
And rain lashed against the rocks night and day,
Until the sea become dull, fetid, and black
Eaten and infested by a deadly plaque.

Those who lost their souls to the sea
Were ferried to Hades to set them free,
Where they morphed at once into beings
Who stared myopically without seeing.

The bottom of the sea bred them forth
To multiply interminably and stay the course
And troll the waters near the stony shore
In search of drowning one or more . . .

Stanzas of the Metaphysical Student Found in a Notebook

Manuel Pérez-Campos

I have come to this squalid holm of misremembering
to study for my exams at the university.
It is an up-piled marginal dank maze of archaic
brownstone: and when it mixes with the imaginary
souvenances required by nightmares it drifts like a vapour
over the rooftops of Paris: notes rayed out by a viol

from a garret spinning under the abyss (a viol
keyed to machine-age angst) annex it to misremembering
though arpeggios that build like an opium vapour
until I misplace where in time is the university
and suspect my desks at dusk there were imaginary
because only those districts of Paris which are archaic

exist—and this garret is anchored in the archaic.
If I should stay within the mannerism of that viol,
and hence opt out of an out there which is imaginary,
I would not have such a need for misremembering
this innhouse courtyard that keeps me from a university
which until fixed on by my psyche must remain a vapour,

nor that bridge which when undertaken renders me a vapour
too, that I may succeed in my flight from the archaic.
Those doctrines I am learning at the university

have helped me counter that feeling directing the viol
of a globe besieged by galaxies: misremembering
the garret from which it hinders the imaginary

is how a Paris addicted to the imaginary
calls me to the defense of factory-billowed vapour
when standing at its belts: it is by misremembering
that the telegraph zeitgeist of scorn for the archaic
turns me from the ether-flumed disclosures of the viol;
and so I seek the colonnades of the university

that I may no longer starve for a university,
having rote-learned the dicta of the imaginary
until I grow wings as its automaton. Though the viol
trill out that one's lifetime is reducible to vapour
and that even Sol's future is doomed to become archaic,
I can pretend all this is false through misremembering.

Let then misremembering be my university.
I sleepwalk past the viol, inured to the archaic:
my maps end in the vapour of the imaginary.

An Apocryphal Addendum to
H. P. Lovecraft's "The Music of Erich Zann"

The Sudden Raving of a Quiet One

John Shirley

Someone's pushing buttons on this madman's sphere
and it's not someone who was born around here—
it's someone from the far side of the universe
(driving an intergalactic hearse)—
Our world is simply his experiment;
he's not any kind of god, he's not heaven sent;
his scientific theory confounds all sense
and if he finds a straight line he'll make it bent.
Our world is the experiment
of an insane scientist
from a star far away;
our world is an experiment
traced with sinister hints
that he'll shut it down
. . . one day.
He's gigantic, he's the size of a god,
and you won't see him 'til even is odd;
he's transparent as a pane of glass—
when the stars align you'll see him at last.
And he'll bring his game to a crashing halt—
and we will point fingers, say it's all our fault;
as all the straight lines forever bend
and the end is the end and the end . . .
is the end.

Procession of the Expendable

David Barker

The King's attendants on his garden isle
Thrash fey palm fronds to cool the royal brow,
While others dance unchaste to raise a smile;
They hope to please their fickle King somehow.
Beloved most are those who twirl at dusk,
Beguiling him with spinning forms sublime,
Their sable locks exuding scents of musk;
Embody they the spirit of this clime.

All pray he'll choose them from among the throng
And raise her status to a queen's, or more,
If only while the moon shines on the hill.
They don't expect to know his passion long
Beyond the time that he'd allot a whore;
Their souls discarded once he's had his fill.

The Stalking Horror

Frank Coffman

With ash-gray skin stretched tight on bony frame,
Red eyes sunk deep in sockets caked with rheum;
With skeletal fingers tipped with razor claws,
An entity that blasphemes Nature's laws:
Gigantic, more than twice a man in height.
It stalks the forests of the frozen night,
Looking for victims at a camp's low flame,
Or digging out a corpse from recent tomb.
All North Tribes fear this horrid, wicked wight—

A taste insatiable for human meat
Drives this dread thing about the wintry wood.
Starvation and grim pestilence mark its realm.
When food is scarce, some folk it lures to eat
The flesh forbidden, savor mankind's blood—
For it is in its power to overwhelm
The mind with thoughts most grisly and abhorrent,
And thus create a creature like itself—
Constantly starving, murderous, fully evil.

Beware those northern forests when the torrent
Of winds and thick snows the dark paths engulf.
O shun the domain of this heinous devil!

But if you venture where no man should go,
And find stripped bones and blood upon the snow;
If, suddenly, you smell the stench of death,
Feel the warm wind of its foetid breath,
Behold the cracked, excoriated lips,
The tongue that, slavering, through those knife fangs slips—
Prepare to die—you've met the Wendigo.

Memoirs in the Dark

Christina Sng

The bones graze my throat
As they go down, scraping
Away the infection.

But too late. It has seeped
Into the core of me,
Changing me permanently.

We fade into the shadows,
Moving into the basement.
The faint glimmer of sun rays,

Our only source of light,
Illuminating the moss gardens
That keep us company and sane

While the cat slips out at night
To patrol and pick fights
With the next door cat.

Sometimes she brings
A bird or a rat.
On that night, we feast

And sleep like cherubs,
Curled up in our wings,
Dreaming of a world

Of darkness and peace,
Without the death touch
Of humanity.

Soon, the only sounds
Are the songs of crickets
And the gentle rumbling

Of thunder
And distant screams
Till the silence drowns out

Everything.
As it does,
Inevitably,

The world falls into chaos
When the apocalypse descends.
I decide then it is time

To rejoin it.

Facing the Demon

Ian Futter

I hide in the half-dark,
alone,
The light flicking fast
between daytime and night.
I stumble in blackness
and groan,
while the foul, flapping beasts
block the sun with their flight.

I shrink at the sound of their
cries,
and cover my ears
from the whispering lies
that predict the promise
of death,
on smothering sighs
from the buffering breath.

Every second I crouch in my
hole
all their sonorous squawks
are a scar to my soul,
so I cower from the scream
and the screech,
fold myself further in,
where I'm far from their reach.

Then I run, as they swipe and they
swoop;
venture out and return,
as if locked in a loop.
I face and then flee from my
fear,
stepping forward and then back,
when vile wings cut the air.

Every day I partake in this
game:
Every week, every year
is exactly the same.
Until one day I leap to the
air,
flap my own fledgling wings,
as the sun disappears.

Volunteers

Ann K. Schwader

Springtime is no time for the dead, & yet
they rise unbidden like any other
perennial. Scented with recollection,
their pallid buds emerge at midnight
in the mind & open slowly
as voices fading. As words regretted
they spread against the moon, each petal
loves me not or loved too late
for more than shadow. Less than cloud
between that cold reflected light
& eyes denied to sleep, their bloom
obscures the certainty of stars
we thought to wish on. To turn back
by will alone one season's haunting.

Hollow of the Night

F. J. Bergmann

Headache again—thrust into my eye socket
like a tongue speaking the language of poison,
a trickle of acid rain swelling a vitreous sac,
its prattle of droplets urging me to wakefulness
in the icy dark, roof creaking under a snow-wight.
It is out there. Silverplate trembles in the cupboard,
or is that the snicketing of fingernails. Every
sound is dyed black and holds its breath.
The ghost of a dead cat sharpens its claws
on moonlight. This is not worth waking for.
I slip between spikes into the oubliette of sleep.

Classic Reprints

The Death Angel

Farnsworth Wright

We struggled in the waves, and I was ware
Of a strange presence moving by my side,
More beautiful than dawn, and dreamy-eyed,
Who half enmesht me with her falling hair,
Blacker than night, yet thousandfold more fair;
And with the siren-voice of dreams she cried:
"Forbear to struggle more, but gently slide
Into my arms: new rapture waits thee there."

To that soft plea I would have yielded then,
But tender voices cried into my ear,
And then the sobs of loved ones I could hear;
And so I turned, and fought the waves again.
My comrade from my side she reft away;
I entered into night, he into day.

[First published in *Weird Tales* 6, No. 3 (September 1925): 387
(as by "Francis Hard").]

To a Young Murderess

Arthur O'Shaughnessy

Fair yellow murderess, whose gilded head
    Gleaming with deaths; whose deadly body white,
Writ o'er with secret records of the dead;
    Whose tranquil eyes, that hide the dead from sight
Down in their tenderest depth and bluest bloom;
    Whose strange unnatural grace, whose prolonged youth,
Are for my death now and the shameful doom
    Of all the man I might have been in truth,

Your fell smile, sweetened still, lest I might shun
    Its lingering murder, with a kiss for lure,
Is like the fascinating steel that one
    Most vengeful in his last revenge, and sure
The victim lies beneath him, passes slow,
    Again and oft again before his eyes,
And over all his frame, that he may know
    And suffer the whole death before he dies.

Will you not slay me? Stab me; yea, somehow,
    Deep in the heart: say some foul word to last,
And let me hate you as I love you now.
    Oh, would I might but see you turn and cast

That false fair beauty that you e'en shall lose,
    And fall down there and writhe about my feet,
The crooked loathly viper I shall bruise
    Through all eternity:—
                Nay, kiss me, Sweet!

[From O'Shaughnessy's *Music and Moonlight: Poems and Songs*
(London: Chatto & Windus, 1874).]

Articles

Verse vs. Free Verse

Frank Coffman

Whether it is accurate to say that traditional rhymed and metered verse is making a sort of "comeback" since the latter part of the twentieth century—with many poets choosing the regularized over the random with regard to rhythm, chimes over chance with regard to rhyme, and traditional over "trendy" with regard to form—it is certainly safe to say that the percentage of poems in traditional form—in rhymed and metered verse—in the weird, horrific, supernatural, and speculative genres is high, and likely higher than in other genres.

It is quite probable that the primary reason for this is, essentially, that modern and contemporary "Poets of the Weird" have followed in the traditions of the sources of early weird and supernatural poetry to be found in the pages of, especially *Weird Tales*, but also other pulp magazines of the great era of the 1920s, '30s, and '40s. Those writers— not only the obvious triumvirate of H. P. Lovecraft, Clark Ashton Smith, and Robert E. Howard, but certainly others, such as Donald Wandrei— whose poetry found its way onto the pages of "The Unique Magazine," were solidly verse poets. They were certainly not alone, but they were part of the Old Guard, holding the line—or at least defiant against—the rising tide of the *vers libre* being championed by "mainstream" poets and critics alike. Of course, we may also look back to Poe, who is rightfully seen as the prime American exponent of the weird in poetry, and we might look a bit further back to Keats ("La Belle Dame sans Merci"), Byron (*Childe Roland*, etc.), Coleridge (*The Rime of the Ancient Mariner*), and likely even back to the poetic Arthurian romances and even to the *Beowulf* poet for the weird in the English tradition. But it should be remembered that all these poets were writing *verse*, all using meter, all but the *Beowulf* poet using full rhyme—although the required alliterations of Anglo-Saxon poetry are a form of rhyme that, in its broadest and most complete definition, is simply the noticeable echo of sound.

I will suggest that a secondary reason for the high percentage of measured and rhymed verse in the genres focused upon in this journal (and many other related magazines, journals, and e-zines today) is *the fact that traditional poetics has merits superior to free verse for the creation, not only of form (which is a given), but also of effective content*. This contention will be itemized and amplified later in this discussion.

It is too easy today for many modern lovers of literature to forget that *free verse* is still in its infancy. It is alive, and it will thrive, but its epoch pales in comparison to the millennia of traditional verse established in all societies and cultures on Earth.

Vers libre was born out of the mistaken notion that fitting patterns, "con-forming" to [forming "with" or "in" traditions] is, in some way, *ipso facto* confining and unduly constraining. Another mistaken premise is the notion that "new forms," or rather "absence of form" (sometimes erroneously called "organicism"), would allow for new thoughts and new ideas that were—in a curious and inexplicable and, ultimately, *indefensible* way—somehow *unutterable* in rhyme or meter. The period from the late nineteenth to the early twentieth century was a time of rebellion against the past and, thus, tradition in the arts in general. Literature, it seems, had to keep pace with her sisters. But it became a time of "change for the sake of change" in the name of what many (maybe most) would still call *liberalism*.

But as G. K. Chesterton has eloquently pointed out, *following traditions is actually one of the most liberal of ideas*. It is absolutely democratic. In *Orthodoxy*, Chapter 4, "The Ethics of Elfland," Chesterton writes:

> Tradition means giving a vote to that most obscure of all classes, our ancestors. It is the democracy of the dead. . . . Tradition refuses to submit to the small and arrogant oligarchy of those who merely happen to be walking about. All democrats object to men being disqualified by the accident of birth; tradition objects to their being disqualified by the accident of death. (85)

All true liberals ("democrats," as Chesterton calls them) would be vehement in their outrage against child abuse also. But so many "babies" have been "thrown out with the bathwater" in the name of free verse that the huge edifice of the poetic past has shuddered significantly with the tremors caused by the *vers libre* movement.

Another great misconception held by and mistake made by the majority of proponents of free verse is *the mystification of the poet as some sort of conduit of the voice of the "goddess"* (as the old Greeks and Romans claimed to believe, while nonetheless actually composing in measured verse). The poet becomes an Aeolian harp through which the divine *afflatus* flows, mystically sounding the strings. The Greek word is *theopneustos*—"god-breathed." One need only wait for the muse and then scrawl down the words that come. And the result will be a poem!

The result of that belief, along with the solid acceptance of the notion that "old" and "past" are always bad and "new" and "current" are always good (or at least better), is what leads would-be "poets" to simply "let the words flow into irregular lines and cadences and intentionally avoid all echoes and rhymes"—and that will be a poem.

Hogwash! We know *true poetry* (whether verse *or* free verse) when we read it or hear it read. We know it by its impact upon our minds and souls. Beyond that we might admire its efficient or even brilliant construction—whether verse *or* free verse. And yet beyond that we might examine and appreciate further the nuances of language and poetic craft that created the achievement of the poem. But it is that "let it flow" mistake—and the resulting plethora of absolutely awful things produced claiming to be poems—that made Frost comment about free verse: "I'd just as soon play tennis with the net down" (*Newsweek*, 30 January 1956, 56).

An Objective Definition of Poetry

Perhaps it would be useful to pin down a definition of *poetry* itself before going further. The world over, *poetry*—as is the case with its counterpart, prose—is an attempt at communication. There are far too many *subjective* definitions of the word. I will try an objective and multipart definition here:
1. Poetry is language to which attention has been paid to the sound of words as well as their sense, to the music of language as well as its meaning.

2. The composer of poetry, the poet, determines the length of line and where the "turn" of the line happens. The word *verse* (from Latin *verso*, "turn") is, thus, in one sense, "a line of poetry." With prose, the writer is not concerned with line endings, but *a poem always displays the same way on a page*. The other—potentially confusing—definition of *verse*, of course, is "poetry that uses meter [a measured rhythm]."

3. Poetry usually makes greater use of *figurative language* than does prose.

4. Poetry usually calls upon the reader's imagination through the creation of *images* [*imagery*] more frequently than does prose.

5. Poetry strives for *concision* and *compactness*, attempting to put a great deal of message and effect into a small package.

I will turn here to a discussion of the value of form itself. Then I will continue by noting and quoting some things that have been said in defense of the newer mode. The points made *for* free verse will be given and, in each case, directly rebutted and debated against.

Finally, some thoughts on the merits of meter, rhyme, and tradition itself will be given, and thoughts upon the peculiar fitness of traditional verse in the creation of the weird, horrific, supernatural, and speculative genres.

The Function of Form

First of all, language itself is *formal*. There are *rules* for all languages on Earth. Grammatical systems are used by tribes in the Amazon or New Guinea or Borneo and other remote regions on the planet where only a small handful or a few hundred speakers get by with only oral communication. Their grammars can be and have been discovered through descriptive linguistics. The major languages have codified such grammatical rules and conventions down from the ancient world through medieval times and the Renaissance up to the current state of modern parlance.

The point is that *form* cannot be avoided. The special cases of intentionally wrenched syntax—as, for example, in some of the poems of e. e. cummings—or in the case of what has been called "abstract" poetry (in which *only sound matters*, the hope being to convey through word-sounds and connotations a sort of feeling or mood), or in the case of "concrete" poetry (in which words are used as graphic or pictorial elements [again as in cummings with such poems as the one about "leaf fall"]), are really outside the range of what most would actually consider "poetry" at all. With these noted exceptions, the poet must still follow the rules of grammar—while being admittedly allowed more freedom (*poetic license*) than the prose writer.

Briefly, this forces most so-called free verse into a conundrum. With the mantra of "Traditional and formal be damned!—too confining, too restrictive of self-expression, too rule-laden, and, in many cases (*inexcusably*) simply too traditional," how does one reconcile the formal requirements of grammar itself?

Whitman's early "free verse" can actually be explained as the use of rhetorical parallelism with *anaphora* (the repeated opening word or phrase) beginning many lines in sequences. Many have compared it to the structures of Hebrew verse to be found in the King James Bible (though Whitman's lines are often exceedingly long). His work is, quite simply, long-line free form, unified by rhetorical parallelism. In some ways, his poetry is essentially blank verse expended, as the rhythms (like all English) tend most often toward the iambic.

Anyone who claim that Dickinson's little poems and tight stanzas are precursors to "free verse" misses the point that she is essentially echoing the ballad stanza of tradition—certainly almost always quatrain stanzas, whatever the rhyme scheme—with the addition of the heavy use of the slant rhyming that she loves and her peculiar use of the dash as, almost, the only punctuation.

Furthermore, most modern *vers libre* poets end up with *distinctive tendencies* in both line divisions that are either words, phrases, or clauses (in other words, elements of grammatical construction) and also in section or even stanza patternings. Their poetry falls into either "short line-," "long line-," or "variable line-length" tendencies. William Carlos Williams actually came up with a grammatical "form" that he favored and used in much of his work—the *Triversen*: "three verse sentence" (see Turco). Many of them come up with even stanza divisions as to number of lines.

So we may ask, "Are these tendencies among so-called 'free verse' poets *not*, in the final analysis, *a return to form, indeed the use of form—even if new and idiosyncratic*, thus reinforcing a possibly innate human preference for and tendency toward form and order?"

And while formalist poetry most often makes use of standard meters and rhyme patterns in stanzas, there are several "fixed forms" that dictate the standards of complete poems rather than building blocks—as a uniform stanza pattern may be considered. To the French these *formes fixes* include only the refrain-laden *ballade, rondeau,* and *virelai,* but most expand this list to include any form that dictates an entire poem structure. Most prominent of these is the sonnet, but it would certainly include the villanelle, the sestina, and standardized forms from any culture or tradition. As Alfred Corn maintains in *The Poem's Heartbeat: A Manual of Prosody,* these forms demand, at the very least "virtuosity": "I think most people would acknowledge that virtuosity, though far from being the greatest value of art, is nevertheless a real value. If we dislike the connotations of the word, then we can substitute for it 'skill,' 'craft,' or mastery" (98–99).

The traditional stanza patterns and fixed forms of English language poetry—in fact, of the poetry of much of the West—include the use of both meter and rhyme. I will defend the uses of both of these later in this essay. But first let us examine what has been said in favor of free verse.

The Concept of Free Verse: Its Postulates and Problems

The urge for more poetic freedom goes back at least as far as Sir Phillip Sidney in his long sonnet sequence of 108 poems, *Astophil and Stella* ["Star-Lover," from the Greek *astro-* and *-phil,* and "Star" from the Latin *stella,* with basis in imitation of Francesco Petrarca's Renaissance sequence of over 300 written to or on his platonic ideal, Laura]. In the famous lament in Sonnet 1 of that sequence, he complains:

> ". . . *Invention, Nature's child, fled step-dame Study's blows;*
> *And others' feet still seem'd but strangers in my way.*
> Thus great with child to speak and helpless in my throes,
> Biting my truant pen, beating myself for spite,
> *'Fool,' said my Muse to me, 'look in thy heart, and write.'"*
> (emphasis added)

Sidney seems to be claiming spontaneity, but he puts it in rhyme in a formal English sonnet (with the slight variation of continuing *abab* in the second quatrain). Though some of the rhythms are ragged and depart from standard iambics, the general meter of the poem is on a framework of alexandrines. This is no true break with tradition at all. The poem mocks itself.

In Matthew Arnold's most famous poem, "Dover Beach," often hailed as a precursor to twentieth-century free verse, we have an example of random rhyme, random line lengths, and slant rhyming. The "rhythm" is actually not at all "free," but rather, in almost every line, measured in standard iambics. It is really an experiment in the randomness of rhyme and line length, in no way a break from the traditions of either.

Stephen Crane, one of the first true experimenters with what must be classed as "free verse," nonetheless used grammatical units as lines: phrase, clauses both dependent and independent.

The tradition of capitalizing the first letters of lines—even with Crane's poetry—continued for all these poets. Showing that traditions are difficult to break. The birth of free verse was painful.

In the twentieth century, poets such as Carl Sandberg were hailed for their *vers libre*, but Sandberg was essentially following Whitman's rhetorical composition and the use of parallelism and repeated line openings.

Certainly, poets throughout the twentieth century and up to the present have used more and more open form, have almost universally eschewed rhyme, and have done away with many of the capitalization and even punctuation rules of tradition. But their poetry, for the most part, displays personal tendencies with regularities—even if idiosyncratic. *In short, most free verse poets create forms of their own, traditions of their own invention, or borrowings from other free-verse poets whom they admire. What is that except for conforming to tradition—albeit new tradition?*

In his preface to *Some Imagist Poets* (1915), Ezra Pound expresses a desire

> . . . *to create new rhythms—as the expression of new moods—and not to copy old rhythms, which merely echo old moods.* We do not insist upon "free-verse" as the only method of writing poetry. We fight for it as for a principle of

liberty. We believe that the individuality of a poet may often be better expressed in free-verse than in conventional forms. *In poetry a new cadence means a new idea.* (vi-vii; emphasis added)

Both of the assertions emphasized in italics above are specious. The notions that "old rhythms" can only express "old moods" or that "a new cadence means a new idea" are both ludicrous. Any kind of communication—whether it be colloquial communication, prose, traditional verse, free verse, or any other variety—might "create" a new mood (that is, if we buy into the questionable premise that *any* "mood" might actually be *new* to human experience). And it should be obvious that any supposedly "new cadence" does not automatically bring with it a "new idea." These are merely poor—indeed, mindless—renditions of the "better because it's new" argument.

Free Verse: Postulates and Rebuttals

1. ARGUMENT: Free Verse (*vers libre*) keeps the traditional forms and conventions of rhymed and metered verse from confining and constraining the creativity and spontaneity of the poet. RESPONSE: *While it is true that many rhymed and metered poems fail due to the versifier's lack of skill/virtuosity with the medium, there are uncounted numbers of traditional poems that clearly show that skilled poets have not been confined or constrained by the use of form.*

2. ARGUMENT: There is never a need to phrase lines awkwardly or ungrammatically to find a rhyme or the right meter. RESPONSE: *While there might be "never a need" to do such phrasing, probably as great a proportion of free verse "poems" fall victim to this as do verse poems. Free verse does not ensure against awkwardness of style or faulty grammar.*

3. ARGUMENT: The poet can let the words flow in a "spontaneous" and "organic" creation. RESPONSE: *Simply letting words flow onto the page is usually called "rough drafting" or "freewriting." Poets are not mystically inspired, superhuman creatures. In fact, the more they are in touch with humanity's truths, the more inspirations come. "Organic" is a curious word—especially in light of the concept of the metaphor as something springing from fertile soil and growing in some typical, traditional, "normal" way. A corn stalk is a corn stalk, a tomato vine a tomato vine—never*

producing bananas. We call variances from organic norms (i.e., forms)–mutations.

4. ARGUMENT: Line endings and line lengths can be used for effect or emphasis. RESPONSE: *This can be just as true of rhymed and metered verse. Random or variable line lengths have nothing to do with meter or its lack. A poem can have monometer up through octameter (or longer) lines and still be iambic. Hopkins's famous sonnet, "The Windhover," shows this in lines one and two: "I caught this morning morning's minion, king- / Dom of daylight's dauphin . . ."*

5. ARGUMENT: The mere breaking with tradition makes a philosophical statement. RESPONSE: *Yes, but one with which many disagree. And a strong defense of the belief that tradition is somehow faulty, wrong, or evil is, ultimately, lacking. If the statement is simply "traditions/old things/the past are bad," then it is too universal–and almost universally untrue.*

6. ARGUMENT: Capitalization and punctuation can be used in non-standard ways to emphasize or add to meaning. RESPONSE: *Nothing that rhymed and metered verse cannot do. Witness Dickinson's heavy use of capital letters (or cummings's general lack of same) and her use of dashes as the non-standard punctuation mark.*

7. ARGUMENT: Grammar can be jumbled as well, if the poet so chooses—in fact, "Abstract Poetry" uses SOUND as the central purpose and often leaves a precise MEANING lacking. The idea, as with music, is to create a mood or feeling with the sounds and connotations (shades of meaning) of words. RESPONSE: *Rhymed and metered verse could do the same. cummings's "anyone lived in a pretty how town" (for one example) illustrates this. Most poets know that tampering with English syntax is risky, since English has dropped most of its ancient inflections and has become syntactic for meaning.*

8. ARGUMENT: "Concrete Poetry" uses words and letters as shapes on the page to emphasize the message or meaning. It is using words as graphic images. RESPONSE: *Some few might "dare," but most would not call that "poetry." It is, rather, an attempt at blending graphics with literature.*

Arguments for Meter, Rhyme, and Tradition

In *The Poet's Handbook*, Judson Jerome writes: "[free verse] is the use of form to create *the illusion of spontaneity*" (159). This is true of much free verse. The idiosyncratically and habitually developed "form" invented by any self-proclaimed "free verse" poet is, ultimately, a pretense at showing off a pretended spontaneous effluence of content. Jerome also argues against the notions of "organicism" and "spontaneity" themselves: "The implication is that one cannot *learn* to write poems. They happen. *The emphasis is not upon craft but upon the nature of the poet, who is a chosen priest or priestess or medium or oracle transmitting a sacred* text" (160–61; emphasis added).

The poet is more of a mechanic with language than a mystic. The poet is not the Aeolian harp through which the goddess of inspiration breathes, but rather an accomplished harpist. The poet is not the instrument, but the musician. Poetry is not innate, but learned. As with any art, it is learned by studying examples. We call those examples *tradition*.

The greatest argument *for* traditional, rhymed, metered verse is the huge edifice of great poetic achievements built through its practice. Verse poets in every land and every language have succeeded in writing excellent poetry for thousands of years in formal and metrical patterns. *This sheer body of quality literature proves that there is nothing* inherently *stifling or confining about verse*. While this general statement, by itself, should suffice, there are specific merits that can be given.

I believe that the single best book on prosody (the techniques of verse) in English is *The Prosody Handbook: A Guide to Poetic Form* by Robert Beum and Karl Shapiro (now back in print in a Dover edition). While most are confused by the notion that "prosody" has to do with poetry and not "prose," the terms derive from different roots. "Prose" derives from a root meaning "straightforward," "direct." "Prosody" derives, ultimately, from the Greek *prosoide*, "a song with accompaniment." The knowledge that poetry and music are sisters is ancient. In that handbook by Shapiro and Beum, there are two chapters especially relevant to the present discussion: "The Uses of Meter" (66–82) and "The Uses of Rhyme" (96–106).

While some of the merits of each are shared by the other, each has some distinctive qualities.

The Uses of Meter

Concerning meter, Beum and Shapiro note the following (I paraphrase and summarize here, for the most part):

1. Meter clearly demonstrates an extraordinary or special use of language, befitting high thought and deep emotion. The world we live in moves in rhythms: the heartbeat, the tides, the cycles of the sun, the changing of the seasons. These rhythms are *regular* in Nature; we say they are *metrical* in poetry. Humans have an innate love of order and regularity.

2. Formality reinforces the concept of orderliness and appropriateness. Form and order are the antitheses of chaos and *dis*-organization.

3. Meter is attention-getting (much like what Tolkien says regarding his first value of Fantasy, as noted in his important essay "On Faerie-Stories," meter has "arresting strangeness"). Due to its far greater formality than the cadences of common speech, the structure itself is interesting. The container can be a supplement to and complement to content.

4. A "sensuous vividness" derives from the regularity of the flow of words. In prose, we tend to race over the words to discover meaning. The full essence of the words is not, generally felt (except in what might be called *prose-poetry* or *highly poetic prose* as with John Donne's "Meditation XVII" or Thomas Paine's opening to *The Crisis*). Words are "more alive" in poetry than in prose—or in *those types of free verse* that approach or, in many cases, indeed *are* prose that is merely arranged differently on the page.

5. Aside from providing *unity* through the repetitive pattern of a meter, the use of meter *allows for distinct and clear metrical variations for emphasis and effect*. The hearer notes changes in rhythm based upon inversion of feet, extrametrical syllables, missing syllables from the normal patterns, and substitutions (like anapest for iamb, for example). These can be used to the poet's advantage and the hearer's pleasure.

6. Meter suggests an artist competent in the medium of expression, a person skilled enough to "whip" even difficult ideas into "shape." Thus, meter can demonstrate virtuosity with literary art. The receiver

of the poem is also more assured that the poet has exercised care and thoughtfulness in crafting the expression.

7. Meter provides *mnemonic value*. It is far easier to memorize lines of metered verse than prose language or free verse. This is why we use meter (and, as will be noted in the next section, rhyme) for adages: "Thirty days hath September, April, June, and November." Or "Columbus sailed the ocean blue / In fourteen hundred and ninety-two." (Of course, the *mnemonic* value of rhyme is present with these as well.) It is far easier to remember the lyrics to a song than the words of a line from a play, for example.

8. And the present writer will add that meter provides a *heuristic* value or function as well. In working and reworking lines to fit a meter (and true poetry is "worked," and not somehow mystically "willed" onto the page), the poet often "finds" the image, the message, and even the direction the poem is going—even to the alteration of initially conceived purpose. *Serendipity more readily strikes those who struggle with form.* She is not the kind spirit sitting beside (residing inside?) the poet, simply breathing out words through the poet's "mouth" or simply guiding the quill.

The Uses of Rhyme

1. Rhyme helps to capture and keep "rapt attention." In is very evidently special language, and the hearer (even if the poem is heard by the "mind's ear") cannot help but notice the exceptional sounds, far different from normal speech or common language. In addition to this, *if some of the rhymed words are "key" words as far as meaning or connotation, then such messages are enhanced.*

2. Rhyme *provides a musical quality* to the message of the poem. There is an *acoustic pleasure* derived beyond any satisfaction of the message or emotional content of the words themselves as meaningful signs. Song lyrics are, almost without exception, rhymed. This is not coincidence. Again, the word *prosoide*, whence "prosody" derives, means "a song with accompaniment." Rhyme is intimately associated with song.

3. Also, as Beum and Shapiro note, *rhyme has a "binding or architectural quality."* This can easily be seen in the two most common types of

sonnet used by English-language poets: the Shakespearean or English sonnet and the Petrarchan or Italian sonnet. The archetypal Italian form divides *by rhyme* into an "octave" and a "sestet": *abbaabba | | cdcdcd* or *cdecde*. These divisions of 8 and 6 traditionally comprise an initial theme or statement and then a response to or refinement of the initial content. The division between the two is usually shown by a space on the page between these two sections at the point of the *volta* (turn). In a similar manner, the initial three quatrains of the English form—*abab | | cdcd | | efef | | gg*—tend to invite the content in the body of the poem to be separated into three divisions of image or thought. The "clincher" couplet at the end is usually used as a summation or final statement. In the same manner, Dante's *Divine Comedy*, composed in *terza rima*, helps to pull the reader forward through the long narrative parts due to the interlocking nature of the stanzas, the unrhymed line in each tercet becoming the main rhyme in the next: *aba | | bcb | | cdc | ded*, etc.

4. Rhyme can be used for emphasis. Rhymed words are conspicuous and their significance is heightened by the repetition of sound (or the expectation of its repetition in the case of normal end-rhyme), since the line cadences of metered verse create a tempo of expectation. Additional rhymes, such as internal rhyme, simply *add to both aural pleasure and emphasis*, as with the internal rhymes of Poe's "The Raven."

5. Rhyme, as does meter, provides a *heuristic* value. A poet chooses a rhyme pattern for a stanza or even a fixed form with a distinct rhyme scheme and is thus *restricted* (but *not "confined" or "constrained"*) by such a decision. That distinction is important. In choosing any typical quatrain stanza (the predominant one in English by far), the choices that include rhyme are the Sicilian quatrain (*abab*), the Italian quatrain (*abba*), the couplet quatrain (*aabb*), some form with three of one and only one of another, such as the rubaiyat stanza (*aaba*), or some form that includes a third sound such as the ballad stanza of tradition (*abcb*). Any other form would not have rhyme. Note that in choosing any of these only one rhymed line (at the most two in the cases of *aaba*, for example) is needed to complete the rhyme effect. In the case of the sonnet or other fixed forms, the need for extra rhymes is, of course, increased (such as the octave of

the Italian sonnet: *abbaabba*). But striving for lines that "work" with the correct rhyming endings very often proves serendipitous to a poet with skill. The decision to rhyme excludes the tens of thousands (conservative number) of possible end words, thus setting the imagination to engage in free association over the still-remaining multitude of options that fit the message or theme. This is stimulus, not constraint. Shoddy verse can result, but shoddy free verse happens at least as often—the result of efforts by a *poetaster* and not a true poet in either form.

6. Rhyme adds formality to language. The hearer knows that the language is meant to be somehow special or more significant.

7. Rhyme aids the poet in achieving "aesthetic distance," as Beum and Shapiro point out. It puts a check on what might be an initial effusion of emotion or an unconsidered statement of thought. In this way, it provides an actual *benefit* that has been seen as a detriment by the exponents of "free verse"—the "let-it-flow" folks. While there may, indeed, be a seemingly mystical component in the creation of a good or great poem, the "goddess" needs to be given some time to "clear her throat" and to reflect upon the experience or chosen theme and then to frame the perfect language for the message.

8. There is no doubt that rhyme provides a *mnemonic* value. It is unquestionably the case that rhyme (likely even to a greater extent than meter, but contributing alongside that element) is more memorable than prose—and more easily memorizable (like song lyrics) than free verse poetry.

Why Traditional Verse May Be More Appropriate in the Weird, Horrific, Supernatural, and Speculative Genres

At the beginning of this essay, I noted that the likely prime reason for the large percentage of rhymed and metered verse in works of contemporary poets in the genres of the weird, horrific, supernatural, and speculative is the tradition of rhymed and metered verse by the chief proponents of these genres who were their great predecessors. It is certain that those earlier poets in these genres who lived in the developing age of the *vers libre* movement from the later nineteenth century onward were almost universally writing, if not in open defiance of the momentum toward free verse (as witnessed in such journals as *Poetry* [Chicago]), then at least in spite of their awareness of that movement.

But there are other considerations that might be seen as making rhymed and metered traditional verse more suitable for these specialized genres. While there are indeed many modern and contemporary poems that are lyrical and self-expressive (especially in the genre that can be properly called simply "speculative"), a great number of poems in the genres of horror, fantasy, adventure, and science fiction—all genres of the high imagination and romance in the old sense—tend to be *narrative* or *descriptive* or even *dramatic*. The first and last of these each *demand the poem as story*. The forms of the ballad and of blank verse have been proven as excellent standards for storytelling in English and also in other languages of the West. They are the staples for that mode. Translations of epics and Shakespeare's plays have often used the unrhymed but metered form. The heroic couplet has also served admirably.

The ballad of tradition (the *folk ballad*) morphed into the *literary ballad* by a single poet a long time ago—and there are no forms easier to rhyme than the ballad, needing only one echo in each stanza in its *abcb* scheme. It is the "common measure" that extends into church hymnals and popular song. Readers are ready for it and primed to enjoy its lilting rhythms.

As Shelley proved beyond doubt with the famous "Ozymandias," the sonnet is not merely a lyric vehicle but can become *the supreme challenge to the poet for the miniaturization of the narrative*. Howard shows this also in his excellent sonnet, "Miser's Gold"; Lovecraft demonstrates it in several of the "micro-stories" in *Fungi from Yuggoth*; and Wandrei earlier proved it in his *Sonnets of the Midnight Hours*.

There is an aptness in the two most often used forms of poetry in our language, the ballad and the sonnet, to be forms of choice and preference for the poet who wishes to write narratives. The sonnet has been used as a sort of verse paragraph on occasion, a series of them continuing a story. Lovecraft does this in the opening sequence to *Fungi from Yuggoth*. Pushkin wrote an entire novel, *Evgenie Onegin* [Евге́ний Оне́гин], as a series of sonnets! These forms are also prime for descriptive poetry (certainly for both *topographia*: writing about a place or location—say, Salem at the time of the witch trials, or Transylvania—and also for *chronographia*: writing about a time or season or event—say,

Halloween). The ballad also invites its other quatrain sisters to be vehicles for longer, more extended poems of any variety.

Of course, the sonnet and other fixed forms such as the villanelle, sestina, etc.—used chiefly for lyric, self-expression by the poet—can be used in these more specialized genres as well.

In conclusion, it has been asserted that there are clear fallacies in the major premises (and also the axioms) of *vers libre*. I have sought to present the values and virtues of meter, rhyme, and traditional verse form and to defend their use and applaud their resurgence and persistency in contemporary poetry—especially in the genres herein considered. It has not been my intent to deprecate all poetry written in the junior form of *vers libre*. Great poems in that mode certainly exist and vast numbers more are certainly yet to be written. Those who appreciate and admire and *write* traditional verse have the luxury of being able to appreciate free verse when it rises to the level of *true poetry*, not having to look askance at the other mode as being of necessity inferior. That openness is also traditional. True poetry will out.

Works Cited

Beum, Robert, and Karl Shapiro. *The Prosody Handbook: A Guide to Poetic Form*. 1965. Mineola, NY: Dover, 2006.

Chesterton, G. K. *Orthodoxy*. 1908. New York: John Lane, 1909.

Corn, Alfred. *The Poem's Heartbeat: A Manual of Prosody*. Port Townsend, WA: Copper Canyon Press, 2008.

Jerome, Judson. *The Poet's Handbook*. Cincinnati: Writer's Digest Books, 1980.

Pound, Ezra. "Preface" to *Some Imagist Poets: An Anthology*. Boston: Houghton Mifflin, 1915. v–viii (unsigned).

Tolkien, J. R. R. "On Fairy-Stories." 1947. In *The Tolkien Reader*. New York: Ballantine, 1966.

Turco, Lewis. *The Book of Forms*. Lebanon, NH: University Press of New England, 2000. (For Turco's comments on the "Triversen." See also: http://lewisturco.typepad.com/poetics/2009/06/william-carlos-williams-prosody.html.)

Reviews

The Exquisite Nightmares of Christina Sng

Sunni K Brock

CHRISTINA SNG. *A Collection of Nightmares*. Bowie, MD: Raw Dog Screaming Press, 2017. 88 pp. $10.95 tpb.

Although Christina Sng may be best known for her Japanese-form poetry (haiku and tanka) and has won several awards for these forms as well as for her science fiction poetry (often combining the theme with the forms previously mentioned), she is certainly well established in the poetry of the dark side. Her most recent book, *A Collection of Nightmares*, is a starkly beautiful assemblage of fantastical verse.

This is a short collection, only 88 pages, but the mastery of style and substance makes for a satisfying read. Indeed, her experience in writing verse gives the feeling that each poem was carved by a sculptor, using language as one would a cutting, to reveal only the elegant, necessary flow of lines that suggest and imprint her gorgeous imagery.

To be sure, the word "exquisite" has been used by many to describe Sng's poetry, and by happenstance this is the title of the first poem in the collection. "Exquisite" is well chosen to open the book: Sng eloquently describes a statue, a once live person frozen in time by the gaze of Medusa. The last line "And then you take a step" is the perfect invitation to step into the remaining pages, to wander about this garden of verse that Sng has so carefully tended.

As we do, looking up, we see skies patrolled by birds of prey, crimson autumn, and the turning of "Seasonal Creatures." Next we encounter a creature who understands the ancient creation of life in

"The Art of Weaving" and, further along the path, a family united in death in "Just as Papa Said."

As the trail unfurls though Sng's world, we find that we aren't in just any garden, but an ancient graveyard filled with ethereal specters and eerie servants of the dark arts. In "The Bone Carver," a cruel boy meets his end after our narrator's brother, Bob, carves a bone effigy and locks it away to suffocate it in revenge for bullying his sister. Again, the passing down of old knowledge through the family is referenced in this poem, and this theme continues through other entries in the collection. As if on cue, the next piece is titled "The Path," and here we find a mother wandering alone through a thick forest with a young girl. It evokes a dreamy state of somnambulance:

> We walk again,
> Hand in hand, down the endless road,
> Slightly limping, but flanked
> By an abundance of fruit trees.

We briefly pause to look through the "Mirror to the Other Side," and as we continue to ponder youth and death in "Resurrection Dreams," we realize we are being watched, even in our slumber, because "They Do Not Sleep." We cannot hide from demons old or new, not even in "Crawlspace," a disturbing slice of personal horrors.

"That Evening" brings a quiet moment, an after-nap pause, before the realization that we are still in the nightmare. Christina Sng gives us her "Confession," and we must listen to her twisting words, even from the safety of "Cocoon" before emerging, stretching our night wings to "The Marvel of Flight." We soar high on this exhilarating ride before plunging wearily into "Dreams of Bone."

A false awakening startles us under the blade of "The Skin Carver," before a Green Fairy dream traps us in "Bottled Quiescence" and we are laid to sleep once more in "Snow Tomb," where we join the carver once more on the path through a landscape of "Bruises," turning pages in this nightmare realm where we succumb to "Death of a Thousand Paper Cuts," in which the author promises:

With time
I will unravel your puzzle,
Unlock the source
Of your dark inclinations,
Tip the scales
Of your volatile mind,
Turn it counterclockwise
And watch you unwind.

Enchanted under Christina Sng's spellbinding lines, we shiver through a "Visitation by Lady Death" and follow our ghost into the sewer, our fears "Fed to Her," until we fall prey to the three acts of "Succubus."

"A Mosquito's Tale" is a flash of lucidity, over in a blink, before we are shrunk back into "The Atomizer and the Matchbox," a cleverly formatted piece that beyond its form functions as a metaphor for Sng's ability to concentrate full thoughts into short lines. "The Confluence" reminds us that we are still asleep, oblivious to the threat of creatures waiting to invade from another realm, accidentally thwarted by our ignorant actions. We laugh at ourselves—then howl—at "Full Moon in Yellowstone" when Jackalopes get their revenge, but "Sleep Takes a Vacation" brings back the echo of the unwaking nightmare.

In this fitful sleep, we examine "Crimes of Our Youth" and are haunted by "Ghost Month," an august setting for summer specters, before turning to "The Fall," in which a great oak tree is felled and the repercussions cascade gracefully and horrifically through this long piece of apocalyptic botanical revenge, continuing as we look up to see the forest sky blackened with "Ravenous" fronds.

From the blackness, we find ourselves in the midst of war on "D-Day" and witness the escape of an alien family from a scorched planet; then we catch up with our little girl again in "Postwar" before we are taken on the beautifully rendered "The Journey." We pause to hear "Ramblings at the End of the World" and meet "Children in the Apocalypse." Exiled for thinking, we join the flight from the mindless zombies in retreat until "After the War," when fairy tales transform and order is restored.

We swim through "Daufin" in a sea dream, emerging onto the sand to witness an ancient brood hatching in "The Awakening," only to return "Underwater" in a science-fictional future. "The Flood" surges forth and we are submerged in blood, wiping our eyes to witness "The Dissection," another wave of epic wars won and grand enemies reduced to fragments. We turn again to "The Monolith" rising from the page, its cosmic indifference leaving us floating in Sng's recursive universe.

"Twenty Years" pass in a spaceship, taking us to "The World's Edge," and our family is outside of time, tending their garden, waiting for the next adventure as we close the book.

In all, this collection is well realized and has an overall feeling of fluid cohesion not unlike that of Magical Realists. Sng excels in various forms while treating us to a hodgepodge of subject matters all woven together through her artful world-building and Japanese sensibilities in both spookiness and elegance of brevity.

If you are a fan of Cosmic Indifference, otherworldly epics, ancient dark arts, and wondering what your cat is thinking, this voyage through Christina Sng's nightmares is time well spent.

Of *Femmes Fatales* and Lost Worlds

Leigh Blackmore

MICHAEL FANTINA. *Alchemy of Dreams and Other Poems.* New York: Hippocampus Press, 2017. 343 pp. $20.00 tpb.

The arrival of Michael Fantina's collection *Alchemy of Dreams* should be greeted with a fanfare and a flourish of trumpets. The sheer size of this gargantuan assemblage of weird and fantastic verse, which has the aura of a magnum opus, puts the many slim volumes published by other weird poets in the shade. Yet bafflingly, the volume includes no introduction by any eminent fellow-poet to usher the reader into

Fantina's glittering worlds of fancy. The publisher's blurb indicates that this is "a generous sampling" of his verse, and so even at such length, this is not the complete Michael Fantina. He must, then, be one of the most prolific of our current crop of weird versifiers, his output only surpassed by such poets as Donald Sidney-Fryer and Bruce Boston.

Fantina's poetic oeuvre has not been as widely acknowledged as it should have been. His first published poem appears to have been "Necromancer's Dream" in *Moonbroth* (1974), and he also published a small collection, *Night Terrors*, that year. Since then he has steadily produced weird and fantastic verse of a high standard, often published in magazines and anthologies in the small press. His work has appeared in *Astral Dimensions, Dark Horizons, Etchings and Odysseys, Eldritch Tales*, the *Lyric*, the *New Formalist, Candelabrum Poetry Magazine, Escape, Space and Time*, the *Pennwood Review, Fantasy Crossroads*, the *Poetry Porch, Fantasy Crosswinds, Sonnet Scroll, Romantics Quarterly, Spectral Realms, Midnight Echo, Contemporary Rhyme*, and many others. He has also published a clutch of short stories.

Yet it has only been a little more than decade since Fantina began to gather his poetic work (which runs the gamut of fantastic themes, from harpies, sirens, and mermaids, to sorcerers, priestesses, and conjurers, to ghosts, death ships, and star travelers), chiefly with the various chapbook collections published by UK's Rainfall Books—*Sirens and Silver* (2006), *Flowers of Nithon* (2009), *This Haunted Sea* (2010), *Ghosts of the Sand* (2013), and most recently *The Strumpet's Eye and Other Poems* (2016).

This impressively weighty new tome of Fantina's poetry from Hippocampus Press ought to enhance his profile overnight. The acknowledgments here credit only four of the poems with previous publication, though in fact some others have appeared prior to this volume—for instance, "Genius Loci" (which appeared in *Midnight Echo* #5) and "The Flying Dutchman" (*Beyond the Borderlands* #2).

Alchemy of Dreams and Other Poems is divided into four major thematic sections: "Vanished Dreams and Lost Worlds" (79 poems); "Down to the Sea in Ships" (57 poems); "Lovers, Ghosts, and Monsters" (90 poems); and "A Wellspring of Arcana" (59 poems). Any one of these would have made an admirable standalone volume. Collected, they make *Alchemy of Dreams* a veritable treasure-house of fantastical verse, a volume not be read cover to cover in order, but dipped into here and there as one would pull out jewels from a pirate's casket, sampling in turn and at random the various riches of Fantina's lush imagination.

"The Sorceress at the End of Space-Time" is nothing if not an epic. Almost six pages in length, it recounts the voyages of the narrator's ghost as it moves through the cosmos on a "nameless quest," encountering various aspects of space—comets, half-dead stars—as well as of Time and Death, finally being confronted by an ancient seer and a lovely beguiling sorceress. The narrator wishes for oblivion, but the final lines tell of the narrator's actual fate:

> Yet death came not, and this I haply tell,
> That she was wed and bonded then to me,
> And for eternity we two may dwell
> Upon this isle, hard by this unknown sea.

Though very much in the vein of such works as George Sterling's "A Wine of Wizardry" and Clark Ashton Smith's *The Hashish-Eater*, Fantina's poem distinguishes itself via the use of rhyme rather blank verse—a feat rarely attempted by other weird poets save Sterling. (See, for example, the poems in *Avatars of Wizardry*, edited by Charles Lovecraft (Sydney: P'rea Press, 2012].) Indeed, even Fantina's epic in that volume, "Sandalwood," is in blank verse, making "The Sorceress at the End of Space-Time" a highly unusual example of rhymed epic.

Another attraction—the icing on the cake, if you will—is several fine illustrations by the UK artist Steve Lines: "The Crystal Flame," "Hippolyte" (looking very much like Xena, Warrior Princess), "The Silent Sea," "Dream Lover," and "The Departure of Malygris." The illustrations apparently don't bear directly on the poems—there is no poem herein entitled "The Departure of Malygris," for instance; but they contribute strongly to making an attractive volume. The appropriately named Lines is certainly among the best of fantasy illustrators today, not excluding such illustrators as Jim Pitts, Allen Koszowski, and Dave Carson. Lines also contributes an effective full-color cover painting of a sorceress. More of his work can be experienced as color covers on his various chapbook series under his own imprint, Rainfall Books (based in Calne, UK).

Fantina's poetry is of almost uniform excellence. He gives a tip of the hat here and there to the oeuvre of weird fiction with such poems as

"Frankenstein" (Mary Shelley) and "Like Queen Mab" (Shakespeare), but such poems are in the minority. He mostly avoids the easy option of drawing upon the imagination of earlier writers via pastiche, preferring to speak in his own voice. It is a voice that rings with magic, yet its music is languid and limpid; there are few Smithian exoticisms or obscurities of language here.

The title poem, "Alchemy of Dreams," consists of seven stanzas of quintain (five lines). The woman, Cassandra, teases and taunts the narrator in his dreams, as he begs her to be his bride but she tells him she's made for no human's bed. She is described as "elflike" and also as a dryad but, as a *femme fatale*, she is also "a savage who works her own will," who "laughs when I beg" and who "schemes and schemes, / She plots and she takes me to dizzy extremes." One can, as is common in work with this type of theme, read either a demonization of the feminine on the narrator's part or his admiration for a woman who stands in her own power.

Elsewhere Fantina effortlessly summons up the lost worlds of Lyonesse, Cockaigne, Ur, Mu, Atlantis, and Nan Modal. (This last is perhaps a transcription error for Nan Madol, the native name of Pohnpei.) Anyone who has ever read and enjoyed such books as L. Sprague de Camp's *Cities and Citadels* or his *Lost Continents*, or Clark Ashton Smith's *Lost Worlds*; anyone who has felt the thrill of contemplating the world of ancient wonders across the centuries prior to our own mundane era, will be enthralled by these poetic evocations of Isfahan and Istanbul, of Rajastan and Zanzibar, and of the (sometimes mythical) distant past.

Although there is a complete contents list, it is a shame that the volume contains no title index or index of first lines. One cannot, then, search for a particular poem by its title except for laboriously searching through the eight-page contents list. Perhaps this may be rectified in a future reprint.

In conclusion, Fantina is a major poet of the weird genre. This is a volume that belongs on the shelf of every connoisseur of weird and fantastic poetry.

Notes on Contributors

Chelsea Arrington has a penchant for things dark and romantic. She loves the poetry of Poe and Swinburne and the stories of Lord Dunsany. Her poetry has appeared in the anthology *Folk Horror Revival: Corpse Roads*. She lives in Southern California with her boyfriend, her nephew, and two lap dogs.

Ross Balcom lives in southern California. His poems have appeared in *Beyond Centauri*, *inkscrawl*, *Poetry Midwest*, *Scifaikuest*, *Star*Line*, and other publications. He is a frequent contributor to *Songs of Eretz Poetry Review*.

David Barker has been a fan of weird literature all his life. Recently, his writings have appeared in *Fungi*, *Cyäegha*, and *Shoggoth.net*. In collaboration with W. H. Pugmire, David has had two books published by Dark Renaissance Books: *The Revenant of Rebecca Pascal* (2014) and *In the Gulfs of Dream and Other Lovecraftian Tales* (2015).

F. J. Bergmann edits poetry for *Mobius: The Journal of Social Change* and imagines tragedies on or near exoplanets. Work appears irregularly in *Analog*, *Asimov's*, *Polu Texni*, *Pulp Literature*, *Silver Blade*, and elsewhere. *A Catalogue of the Further Suns*, a collection of dystopian first-contact poems, won the 2017 Gold Line Press poetry chapbook contest and is available at fibitz.com.

Leigh Blackmore has written weird verse since age thirteen. He has lived in the Illawarra, New South Wales, Australia, for the last decade. He has edited *Terror Australis: Best Australian Horror* (1993) and *Midnight Echo 5* (2011) and written *Spores from Sharnoth & Other Madnesses* (2008). A nominee for SFPA's Rhysling Award (Best Long Poem), Leigh is also a four-time Ditmar Award nominee. He is currently assembling an edition of *The Selected Letters of Robert Bloch*.

Benjamin Blake was born in 1985 and grew up in the small town of Eltham, New Zealand. He is the author of the poetry and prose collections *A Prayer for Late October, Southpaw Nights*, and *Reciting Shakespeare with the Dead*. His debut novel, *The Devil's Children*, was published in October 2016.

Adam Bolivar, a native of Boston, now residing in Portland, Oregon, has had his weird fiction and poetry appear in the pages of *Nameless*, the *Lovecraft eZine*, *Spectral Realms*, and Chaosium's *Steampunk Cthulhu* and *Atomic Age Cthulhu* anthologies. His latest collection, *The Lay of Old Hex*, was published in 2017 by Hippocampus Press.

Sunni K Brock's fiction and poetry combines science fiction, horror, fantasy, and erotica. As one-half of the team of JaSunni Productions, LLC and Cycatrix Press, she creates genre film and print with her husband, Jason.

Frank Coffman is professor of English, journalism, and creative writing at Rock Valley College in Rockford, Illinois. His primary interests as a critic are in the rise and relevance of popular imaginative literature across the genres of adventures, detection and mystery, fantasy, horror and the supernatural, and science fiction. He has published several articles on these genres and is the editor of Robert E. Howard's *Selected Poems*.

Ashley Dioses is a writer of dark fiction and poetry from southern California. Her fiction and poetry has appeared in *Weird Fiction Review*, *Spectral Realms*, *Xnoybis*, *Weirdbook*, *Gothic Blue Book*, and elsewhere. Her debut collection of dark traditional poetry, *Diary of a Sorceress*, was published in 2017 by Hippocampus Press.

J. T. Edwards was born and raised, where he still resides, in East Tennessee. He found solace in the weird and macabre at a young age, watching shows such as *The Twilight Zone*. His later discovery of the works of H. P. Lovecraft, Clark Ashton Smith, Thomas Ligotti, and Austrian expressionist poet Georg Trakl, to name a few, proved monumental in keeping him going through dark times and furthering his imagination.

Poems by **Kendall Evans** have appeared in *Weird Tales, Analog, Asimov's*, and other magazines. His stories have appeared in *Amazing, Weirdbook*,

Fantastic, and elsewhere. His novel *The Rings of Ganymede,* a ring cycle in the tradition of Wagner's operas and Tolkien's *Lord of the Rings,* is now available (Alban Lake Books, 2014).

Ian Futter began writing stories and poems in his childhood, but only lately has started to share them. One of his poems appears in Jason V Brock's anthology *The Darke Phantastique* (Cycatrix Press, 2014), and he continues to produce dark fiction for admirers of the surreal.

Joshua Gage is an ornery curmudgeon from Cleveland. He is the author of five collections of poetry. His newest chapbook, *Necromancy,* is available on Locofo Chaps from Moria Press. He is a graduate of the Low Residency MFA Program in Creative Writing at Naropa University. He has a penchant for Pendleton shirts and any poem strong enough to yank the breath out of his lungs.

Liam Garriock is an author and poet who counts authors such as Kafka, Arthur Machen, J. G. Ballard, Lovecraft, William S. Burroughs, Borges, Poe, William Blake, and Philip K. Dick as among his many touchstones. He lives in Edinburgh, Scotland.

Wade German is the author of *Dreams from a Black Nebula* (Hippocampus Press, 2014). His poetry has been nominated for the Pushcart, Rhysling, and Elgin awards, and has received numerous honorable mentions in Ellen Datlow's *Best Horror of the Year* anthologies.

Alan Gullette is a poet and author whose work has appeared in three dozen amateur and small-press publications, including *Arkham Sampler, Crypt of Cthulhu, Cthulhu Codex, Etchings and Odysseys, Nyctalops,* and *Studies in Weird Fiction.* Hippocampus Press published his omnibus *Intimations of Unreality* in 2012.

Will Hart, whose California license plate is "CTHULHU," has collected, performed, photographed, recorded, shared, and written about all things Lovecraftian for nearly fifty years; and he is most proud of recently being the voice of Fedogan & Bremer's CD of H. P. *Lovecraft's Fungi from Yuggoth and Other Poems.* "Pumpkin, Oh Pumpkin!" is Will's first published poem.

Charles Lovecraft is a resident of Sydney, where he studies English at Macquarie University. He started writing in 1972, inspired by George Orwell. He began writing in earnest in 1975, inspired momentously by H. P. Lovecraft. As publisher-editor, Charles began P'rea Press in 2007 to publish weird and fantastic poetry, criticism, and bibliography, and to keep traditional poetry forms alive (www.preapress.com). He has edited thirty-one books.

Rob Matheny is a writer, voice actor, and producer based out of Salem, Oregon. He is a longtime fan of dark speculative fiction, founder of the Grimdark Fiction Readers & Writers Facebook group, and cohost of the Grim Tidings podcast. As a relative newcomer to poetry, Rob's work focuses on the macabre, the occult, and the strange.

K. A. Opperman is a poet with a predilection for the strange, the Gothic, and the grotesque, continuing the macabre and fantastical tradition of such luminaries as Poe, Clark Ashton Smith, and H. P. Lovecraft. His first verse collection, *The Crimson Tome*, was published by Hippocampus Press in 2015.

Manuel Pérez-Campos's poetry has appeared previously in *Spectral Realms* and is forthcoming in *Weird Fiction Review*. A collection of his poetry in the key of the weird is in progress; so is a collection of groundbreaking essays on H. P. Lovecraft. He lives with his two cats in Bayamón, Puerto Rico.

Shawn Ramsey is a professor of rhetoric and writing in Wenzhou, Zheijang Province, China. He has two children and a Ph.D. in rhetoric and writing, as well as a J.D. He has been a poet for twenty-seven years and published a magazine of strnage poetry, the *Spectre*, and co-edited the journal *Revelations from Yuggoth* with Robert M. Price. He has written numerous articles on the topic of rhetoric but is currently interested in the history of writing.

John Reinhart is an arsonist, father of three, and poet. He was the recipient of the 2016 Horror Writers Association Dark Poetry Scholarship, and he has been a Pushcart, Rhysling, and Dwarf Stars award nominee. To date, he has written five collections of poetry, with a sixth (*Arson*) out in early 2018 from NightBallet Press.

Recent books by **Jessica Amanda Salmonson** include *The Weird Epistles of Penelope Pettiweather, Ghost Hunter* (Alchemy Press), *The Death Sonnets* (Rainfall), and *Pets Given in Evidence of Old English Witchcraft and Other Bewitched Beings* (Sidecar Preservation Society). She has recently contributed novelettes, short stories, and poems to *Weird Tales, Weirdbook, The Audient Void, Space & Time, Skelos*, etc. Her Ace Books trilogy *The Tomoe Gozen Saga* has recently come back into print from Open Road Media as audiobooks and ebooks.

David Schembri has been published in several print anthologies and magazines. He is also the author of *Unearthly Fables*, an illustrated collection of short horror stories. Two of his poems will be appearing in a forthcoming anthology from Rainfall Books.

Ann K. Schwader lives and writes in Colorado. Her most recent collections are *Dark Energies* (P'rea Press, 2015) and *Twisted in Dream* (Hippocampus Press, 2011). Her *Wild Hunt of the Stars* (Sam's Dot, 2010) and *Dark Energies* were Bram Stoker Award finalists. She is also a two-time Rhysling Award winner (2010 and 2015) and was the Poet Laureate for NecronomiCon Providence 2015.

Darrell Schweitzer is a short story writer and novelist, and former coeditor of *Weird Tales*. He has published much humorous Lovecraftian verse (*Non Compost Mentis* [Zadok Allen, 1993] et al.) and also has two serious poetry collections in print, *Groping toward the Light* (Wildside Press, 2000) and *Ghosts of Past and Future* (Wildside Press, 2008).

John Shirley is the author of numerous novels and books of short stories. His latest novel is *Doyle After Death* (HarperCollins, 2013), a tale of Sir Arthur Conan Doyle in the afterlife. He won the Bram Stoker Award for his story collection *Black Butterflies*.

Claire Smith's poetry has appeared, most recently, in journals and anthologies including earlier editions of *Spectral Realms, Illumen*, and *Trysts of Fate*. Her most recent publication was in the gender-themed e-journal *Eye to the Telescope*, with the poem "Account from the Waiting Craft." She lives in Cheltenham, Gloucestershire, U.K., with her husband and their Tonkinese cat.

Oliver Smith is a visual artist and writer from Cheltenham, UK. His poetry has appeared in *Spectral Realms, Eye to the Telescope*, and *Weirdbook*. His collection of strange sea stories, *Stars Beneath the Ships*, was published by Ex Occidente Press in 2017, and many of his previously anthologised stories and poems are available in the collection *Basilisk Soup and Other Fantasies*. He is currently studying for a Ph.D. at the University of Gloucestershire.

Christina Sng is a poet, writer, and artist. Her work has appeared in numerous venues worldwide and garnered nominations in the Dwarf Stars and Rhysling Awards, as well as honorable mentions in *The Year's Best Fantasy and Horror*. She is the author of *A Collection of Nightmares*, *Astropoetry*, and Elgin nominee *An Assortment of Sky Things*.

Richard L. Tierney's *Collected Poems* appeared from Arkham House in 1981. A later volume of poetry was published as *Savage Menace and Other Poems of Horror* (P'rea Press, 2010). Tierney is also the author of *The Winds of Zarr* (Silver Scarab Press, 1975), *The House of the Toad* (Fedogan & Bremer, 1993), and many other works of horror and fantasy fiction.

Don Webb, who has been nominated for the Rhysling Award and the International Horror Critics Award, is the principal of the women's high school in the Lockhart Work Project. He has a new full-length poetry collection, *From Deep Dendo*, available from Dunhams Manor Press. He teaches horror writing for UCLA Extension.

M. F. Webb's poetry has appeared in previous issues of *Spectral Realms* and her fiction in *Latchkey Tales*. She hails from a Victorian seaport town not too far from Seattle, from which she has not yet seen the spectre of the *Mary Celeste*.

Abigail Wildes is a gothic poet and writer whose work has appeared in *Obscurum 2: The Death Issue* and *Merchants of Misery: Authors Against*

Addiction. She is currently working on a collection of New Gothic Poetry and *The Sad Little Tales of Annabelle Lee.*

Mary Krawczak Wilson has written poetry, fiction, plays, articles, and essays. She was born in St. Paul, Minnesota, and moved to Seattle in 1991. Her most recent essay appeared in the *American Rationalist.*

CPSIA information can be obtained
at www.ICGtesting.com
Printed in the USA
BVHW04s0336280318
511787BV00020B/353/P